RV Camping in
National Parks

Published by:

Roundabout Publications
PO Box 569
LaCygne, KS 66040

800-455-2207

www.RoundaboutPublications.com

Published by:

Roundabout Publications
PO Box 569
LaCygne, KS 66040

Phone: 800-455-2207
Internet: www.RoundaboutPublications.com

Library of Congress Control Number: 2018964479

ISBN-10: 1-885464-71-1
ISBN-13: 978-1-885464-71-2

Contents

Introduction

The National Park Service

On August 25, 1916, President Woodrow Wilson approved legislation creating the National Park Service, a new federal bureau in the Department of Interior. Its responsibility was to protect the 35 national parks and monuments in existence at the time and those yet to be established. Today the National Park Service is made up of more than 400 areas encompassing over 84 million acres.

About This Book

This book describes all of the RV camping opportunities available in parks managed by the National Park Service. It not only includes National Parks but also National Seashores, National Monuments, National Recreation Areas, and others.

At the beginning of each state chapter, you'll find a map with the National Park Service areas shown within the state. This allows you to easily see where each park is located within the state. Detailed information follows the map.

Details for each park include contact information, a brief description of the park's features, official scenic drives (if any), the location of visitor centers, entrance fees and season of operation, driving directions, and detailed RV campground information. Visitor centers have free maps, brochures, and park rangers available to answer your questions.

Campground details for each park include location, season of operation, number of sites, and cost per night. You'll also find a list of amenities and facilities available such as restrooms, dump stations, showers, and more. RV length limits, if known, are provided as are length of stay restrictions. Reservation information is also provided if the campground has sites that can be reserved in advance.

Additional Information

Be sure to look at the appendices for additional information about the National Park Service. In Appendix A you'll find information about America the Beautiful discount passes. Appendix B describes the various designations assigned to National Park Service areas such as national parks, national monuments, national recreation areas, etc. In Appendix C you'll find information about visiting parks with your pet. Appendix D is a list of National Park Service campgrounds that are free.

Alaska

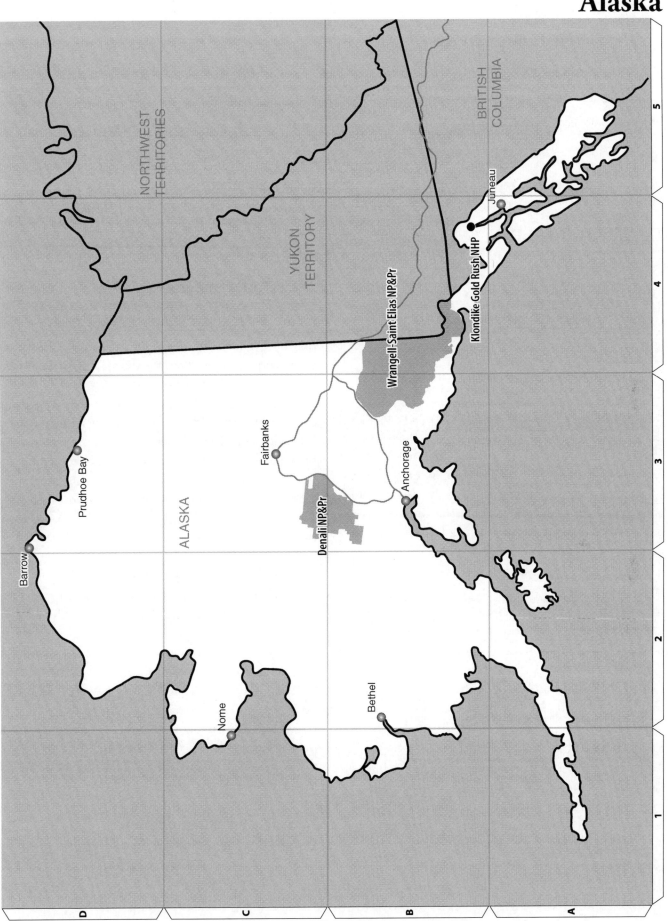

NORTHWEST TERRITORIES

YUKON TERRITORY

BRITISH COLUMBIA

ALASKA

Barrow

Prudhoe Bay

Fairbanks

Nome

Bethel

Anchorage

Denali NP&Pr

Wrangell-Saint Elias NP&Pr

Klondike Gold Rush NHP

Juneau

D

C

B

A

1

2

3

4

5

Alaska Parks

	Map	Auto Touring	Biking	Boating	Climbing	Fishing	Hiking	Horseback Riding	Hunting	Snow Skiing	Swimming	Visitor Center	Wildlife Viewing
Denali National Park & Preserve	C3	•	•		•	•	•		•	•		•	•
Klondike Gold Rush National Historical Park	B4		•	•		•	•	•	•		•		• •
Wrangell-Saint Elias National Park & Preserve	B4	•	•		•	•	•	•	•	•		•	•

PARK DETAILS

Denali National Park & Preserve

PO Box 9
Denali Park AK 99755
Phone: 907-683-9532

Description

Denali National Park and Preserve is home to 20,320-foot Mount McKinley, North America's highest peak. Established in 1917 as Mount McKinley National Park, the park was originally designated a wilderness area. In 1980 it was incorporated into Denali National Park and Preserve. The park encompasses over six million acres. Private vehicle access is restricted to the first 15 miles of Denali Park Road. To travel farther into the park, shuttle and tour bus services are available. Bicycles are permitted along the Park Road.

Information

Information is available from two visitor centers. Denali National Park Visitor Center is 1.5 miles inside the park and is open 8am to 6pm, mid-May to mid-September. Eielson Visitor Center is at mile 66 of Denali Park Road and is open 9am to 7pm, June to mid-September; it can only be reached by shuttle bus.

Fees & Season

An entrance fee of $15 per person is charged. Although the park remains open year-round, summer is when most visitors come. Most summer visitor services and activities are available mid-May to mid-September.

Directions

There is only one entrance into the park, which is located along Alaska Highway 3 (also known as the George Parks Highway) about 240 miles north of Anchorage or 120 miles south of Fairbanks.

RV CAMPING

Riley Creek Campground

Located near the park entrance. Open all year, 107 sites with picnic tables and fire grates, $24 to $30 per night, drinking water, flush and vault toilets. A general store, showers, laundry, and dump station are nearby. Camping is free mid-September to mid-May when facilities are limited. Pets welcome. The campground can accommodate RVs up to 40 feet at some sites. There is a 14-day stay limit. Reservations are accepted and can be made online at reservedenali.com or by calling 800-622-7275. If you do not have advance reservations, plan to camp outside the park when you first arrive. There may be a two-night wait for a campsite within the park.

Savage River Campground

Located at mile 13 of Park Road. Open mid-May to mid-September, 32 sites with picnic tables and fire grates, $24 to $30 per night, drinking water, flush and vault toilets. Pets welcome. The campground can accommodate RVs up to 40 feet at some sites. There is a 14-day stay limit. Reservations are accepted and can be made online at reservedenali.com or by calling 800-622-7275. If you do not have advance reservations, plan to camp outside the park when you first arrive. There may be a two-night wait for a campsite within the park.

Teklanika River Campground

Located at mile 29 of Park Road. Open mid-May to mid-September, 53 sites with picnic tables and fire grates, $25 per night, drinking water, restrooms with flush toilets. RVers planning to stay in this campground are required to stay a minimum of three nights. Pets welcome. The campground can accommodate RVs up to 40 feet at some sites. There is a 14-day stay limit. Reservations are accepted and can be made online at reservedenali.com or by calling 800-622-7275. If you do not have advance reservations, plan to camp outside the park when you first arrive. There may be a two-night wait for a campsite within the park.

PARK DETAILS

Klondike Gold Rush National Historical Park

PO Box 517
Skagway, AK 99840
Phone: 907-983-9200

Description
Klondike Gold Rush National Historical Park celebrates the Klondike Gold Rush of 1897-98 through numerous restored buildings within the Skagway Historic District. The park also preserves a portion of the Chilkoot and White Pass Trails and the Dyea Townsite at the foot of Chilkoot Trail. A permit is required to hike the U.S. and Canadian portions of the Chilkoot Trail. More than a million people visit this park each year.

Information
Information is available from the visitor center inside the restored railway depot building at Broadway and Second Avenue. The center is open daily between 8am and 6pm from early May to late September.

Fees & Season
There is no entrance fee, however fees are charged for using the campground and hiking the Chilkoot Trail. The park remains open year-round but some exhibits and services are closed in winter.

Directions
Klondike Gold Rush National Historical Park is in southeast Alaska in Skagway, which is situated at the northernmost point of the Inside Passage in southeast Alaska. It is located 96 air miles north of Juneau or 110 highway miles south of Whitehorse, Canada.

RV CAMPING

Dyea Campground
Located nine miles from Skagway near the old townsite of Dyea. Open when free of snow, 22 sites with picnic tables and fire grates, $10 per night, pit toilets. Visitors are advised to bring drinking water and firewood. Sites are available on a first-come, first-served basis; reservations are not accepted.

PARK DETAILS

Wrangell-Saint Elias National Park & Preserve

Mile 106.8 Richardson Hwy
PO Box 439
Copper Center, AK 99573
Phone: 907-822-5234

Description
This 13.2 million acre park (America's largest national park) is located in southeast Alaska. Here, the Chugach, Wrangell, and Saint Elias mountain ranges converge. The park contains America's largest collection of glaciers and mountains above 16,000 feet. Mount Saint Elias, at 18,008 feet, is the second highest peak in the United States. Around 66,000 visitors come to the park annually in search of a unique wilderness experience.

Information
Visitor information is available from the Wrangell-Saint Elias Visitor Center, which is located at mile 106.8 on Richardson Highway. It remains open daily from 9am to 6pm in the summer and is closed November through March. Information is also available from the Kennecott Visitor Center (open Memorial Day through Labor Day), which is located in the historic general store within the Kennecott Mill Town. Information may also be obtained from the McCarthy Road Information Station at mile 59 and two ranger stations.

Fees & Season
There is no entrance fee. The park remains open all year although services may be limited in winter.

Directions

Wrangell-Saint Elias is located in southeast Alaska about 200 miles east of Anchorage. The park's headquarters is located along Richardson Highway about 10 miles south of Glennallen.

RV CAMPING

Kendesnii Campground

Located at mile 27.8 on Nabesna Road. Open year-round, 10 sites with picnic tables and fire rings, free, vault toilets. Pets welcome. The campground can accommodate small and medium sized RVs. Sites are available on a first-come, first-served basis; reservations are not accepted.

Arizona

UTAH

CO

NEVADA

15

Glen Canyon NRA

89

Navajo NM ●

160

Lake Mead NRA
(see Nevada)

NM

Grand Canyon NP

Canyon de Chelley NM

93

89

D

40

Sunset Crater Volcano NM ●

Kingman

Flagstaff

40

191

ARIZONA

93

77

260

17

CALIFORNIA

Springerville

C

87

60

93

70

10

Phoenix

79

77

8

10

B

Yuma

10

10

Tucson

Organ Pipe Cactus NM

Chiricahua NM ●

19

A

*Gulf of
California*

MEXICO

1   2   3   4

Arizona Parks

	Map	Auto Touring	Biking	Boating	Climbing	Fishing	Hiking	Horseback Riding	Hunting	Snow Skiing	Swimming	Visitor Center	Wildlife Viewing
Canyon De Chelly National Monument	D4	•					•	•				•	
Chiricahua National Monument	B4	•					•					•	•
Glen Canyon National Recreation Area	E3	•	•	•		•	•				•	•	•
Grand Canyon National Park	D2	•	•	•		•	•	•				•	•
Lake Mead National Recreation Area - *see Nevada*	D1	•	•	•		•	•	•	•		•	•	•
Navajo National Monument	E3						•					•	•
Organ Pipe Cactus National Monument	B2	•	•		•		•	•				•	•
Sunset Crater Volcano National Monument	D3						•					•	

PARK DETAILS

Canyon de Chelly National Monument

PO Box 588
Chinle, AZ 86503
Phone: 928-674-5500

Description

Canyon de Chelly National Monument lies within the Navajo Reservation about 200 miles northeast of Flagstaff. The nearly 84,000-acre park contains ruins of Indian villages constructed between 350 and 1300 A.D. Paved roads within the park lead to various overlooks on the north and south sides of the canyon. Private tours into the canyon by hiking, horseback, or vehicle are offered and require a backcountry permit and hiring an authorized guide. There is one public hiking trail on the South Rim at the White House Overlook. This trail takes the visitor 600 feet down to the White House Ruin.

Information

Information is available from the Canyon de Chelly Visitor Center, located three miles east of US-191 in Chinle. The visitor center is open daily year-round (except for Thanksgiving, Christmas, and New Year's Day) from 8am to 5pm and has exhibits featuring the cultural history of the area.

Fees & Season

No entrance fee is charged. Fees are charged if staying overnight in the campground, for backcountry permits, and canyon tours. The park remains open all year.

Directions

Canyon de Chelly is about 215 miles northeast of Flagstaff via I-40 and US-191. The park's visitor center and primary entrance is three miles east of US-191 in Chinle.

RV CAMPING

Cottonwood Campground

Located near the visitor center. Open all year, 93 sites with picnic tables and fire grates, $14 per night, drinking water, restrooms with flush toilets, dump station. Limited facilities in winter. Pets welcome. The campground can accommodate RVs up to 40 feet at some sites. There is a 14-day stay limit. Sites are available on a first-come, first-served basis; reservations are not accepted. Campground is managed by the Navajo Parks and Recreation Department.

PARK DETAILS

Chiricahua National Monument

12856 E Rhyolite Creek Rd
Willcox, AZ 85643
Phone: 520-824-3560

Description

Chiricahua National Monument preserves nearly 12,000 acres of the Chiricahua Mountains and unusual rock formations. The park features an eight-mile scenic drive and 17 miles of hiking trails. There is no food service, gasoline, or lodging within the park; supplies should be obtained in Willcox before venturing into the park. There is one road within the park, Bonita Canyon Drive, which provides access to numerous overlooks, picnic areas, and hiking trails. The paved road ends at Massai Point. Vehicles longer than 29 feet are not permitted in the campground or beyond the visitor center.

Information

Information is available from Chiricahua Visitor Center located two miles from the park's entrance. It is open daily all year from 8am to 4:30pm (except Thanksgiving and Christmas Days) and has audiovisual programs, exhibits, and books for sale.

Fees & Season

No entrance fee is charged. The park is open year-round but the park road and portions of the campground can be temporarily closed due to hazardous conditions such as monsoon flooding and related debris flows.

Directions

Chiricahua National Monument is in southeast Arizona about 36 miles southeast of Willcox via SR-186 and SR-181. Willcox is located off I-10 at Exit 340.

RV CAMPING

Bonita Canyon Campground

Located about 2.5 miles east of the park's entrance. Open all year, 25 sites with picnic tables and fire grates, $20 per night, drinking water, restrooms with flush toilets. Pets welcome. The campground can accommodate RVs up to 29 feet at some sites. There is a 14-day stay limit. Reservations are accepted and can be made online at recreation.gov or by calling 877-444-6777. The campground is busiest in spring and fall and typically fills every night.

PARK DETAILS

Glen Canyon National Recreation Area

PO Box 1507
Page, AZ 86040
Phone: 928-608-6200

Description

Glen Canyon National Recreation Area is located in northern Arizona and southern Utah. The park encompasses over 1.2 million acres and was established in 1972. Lake Powell stretches 186 miles behind Glen Canyon Dam and is the park's main attraction. More than two million visitors come to the park each year.

Information

Information is available from two visitor centers. Bullfrog Visitor Center is 86 miles south of Hanksville, Utah, via SR-95 and SR-276. The visitor center is open intermittently beginning in May; call 435-684-7423 for hours. Carl Hayden Visitor Center is located at Glen Canyon Dam on US-89 in Page, Arizona, and remains open year-round except winter holidays.

Fees & Season

An entrance fee of $30 per vehicle is charged. Additional fees are charged for boating/vessel permit, ferry charges, dam tours, and other commercial tours. Glen Canyon National Recreation Area remains open all year but some services are limited in winter.

Directions

The park's headquarters is located in Page, Arizona, south of Glen Canyon Dam and the Carl Hayden Visitor Center. Page is located approximately 130 miles north of Flagstaff via US-89.

RV CAMPING

Bullfrog RV Park & Campground

Concession-operated campground in Utah about 86 miles south of Hanksville via SR-95 and SR-276. Open all year, 24 sites with full hookups (30 amp power), picnic tables and fire grates, $50 per night, drinking water, restrooms with flush toilets, showers. Pets welcome. The campground can accommodate RVs up to 50 feet. There is a 14-day stay limit. Reservations are accepted and can be made online at lakepowell.com or by calling 435-684-3032.

Halls Crossing RV Park & Campground

Concession-operated campground in Utah 87 miles west of Blanding via SR-95 and SR-276. Open all year, 32 sites with full hookups, picnic tables and fire grates, $48 per night, drinking water, restrooms with flush toilets, showers. Pets welcome. The campground can accommodate RVs up to 60 feet. There is a 14-day stay limit. Reservations are accepted for RV sites and can be made online at lakepowell.com or by calling 435-684-7008.

Hite RV Campground

Remote concession-operated campground in Utah about 92 miles south of I-70 Exit 149. Open year-round, eight sites with full hookups (50 amp power), picnic tables and fire grates, $46 per night, drinking water, restrooms with flush toilets, camp store, dump station nearby. Pets welcome. The campground can accommodate large RVs. There is a 14-day stay limit. Sites are available on a first-come, first-served basis; reservations are not accepted.

Lees Ferry Campground

Located in Arizona about five miles north of Marble Canyon off US-89-ALT. Open year-round, 54 sites with picnic tables and grills, $20 per night, drinking water, restrooms with flush toilets, dump station. Open fires prohibited. Pets welcome. The campground can accommodate RVs up to 35 feet at some sites. There is a 14-day stay limit. Sites are available on a first-come, first-served basis; reservations are not accepted.

Wahweap RV Park & Campground

Concession-operated campground in Arizona about four miles north of Glen Canyon Dam off US-89. Open all year, 139 sites with full hookups ($52 per night, 70-foot RV length limit), 112 no-hookup sites ($30 per night, 40-foot RV length limit), drinking water, restrooms with flush toilets, dump station, showers, laundry, groceries. Pets welcome. There is a 14-day stay limit. Reservations are accepted and can be made online at lakepowell.com or by calling 435-684-3032. Free Wi-Fi is available at the campground but connectivity varies.

PARK DETAILS

Grand Canyon National Park

PO Box 129
Grand Canyon, AZ 86023
Phone: 928-638-7888

Description

Grand Canyon National Park encompasses 277 miles of the Colorado River and 1.2 million acres of land in northern Arizona. The canyon reaches a width of 18 miles and a depth of one mile. The park is one of few designated an International Dark-Sky Park. More than four million people visit the park annually; visitation is highest in spring, summer, and fall. Reservations for camping and lodging are essential during this time.

Information

There are four visitor center locations within the park. The Grand Canyon Visitor Center is on the South Rim by Mather Point and is open daily from 8am to 5pm. Verkamp's Visitor Center is just east of the El Tovar Hotel on the South Rim; it is open in summer between 8am and 8pm. Desert View Visitor Center is 25 miles east of Grand Canyon Village on the South Rim and is open daily from 9am to 6pm. The North Rim Visitor Center is open daily from mid-May to mid-October between 8am and 6pm.

Fees & Season

An entrance fee of $35 per vehicle is charged. The fee is good for seven days and includes entrance to both South Rim and North Rim. Camping fees are in addition to the entrance fee. The South Rim is open all year. All visitor services are available year-round. The

North Rim is typically open from mid-May to mid-October. There is a period when the North Rim is open for day use through December 1st or until snow closes SR-67.

Directions

Entrance to the South Rim is about 52 miles north of Williams, Arizona, and I-40 Exit 165 via SR-64. The North Rim is reached by following SR-67 for approximately 44 miles south of US-89A.

RV CAMPING

Desert View Campground

Located 26 miles east of Grand Canyon Village on the South Rim. Open mid-April to mid-October, 50 sites with picnic tables and fire grates, $12 per night, drinking water, restrooms with flush toilets. Pets welcome. The campground can accommodate RVs up to 30 feet at some sites. There is a 7-day stay limit. Sites are available on a first-come, first-served basis; reservations are not accepted. The campground typically fills by noon.

Mather Campground

Located in Grand Canyon Village on the South Rim. Open all year, 318 sites with picnic tables and fire grates, $18 per night ($15 in winter), drinking water, restrooms with flush toilets. Showers, laundry, and a dump station are nearby. Pets welcome. The campground can accommodate RVs up to 30 feet at some sites. There is a 7-day stay limit. Reservations are accepted and can be made online at recreation.gov or by calling 877-444-6777.

Trailer Village RV Park

Concession-operated campground located adjacent to Mather Campground. Open all year, 78 sites with full hookups (30 and 50 amp power), picnic tables and fire grates, $41-$45 per night, drinking water, restrooms with flush toilets. Showers, laundry, and a dump station are nearby. Pets welcome. The campground can accommodate RVs up to 50 feet at some sites. There is a 7-day stay limit. Reservations are accepted and can be made online at visitgrandcanyon.com or by calling 877-404-4611.

North Rim Campground

Located along SR-67 on the North Rim. Open mid-May through October, 78 sites with picnic tables and fire grates, $18 to $25 per night, drinking water, restrooms with flush toilets, dump station. Coin-operated laundry and showers are located at the campground entrance. Pets welcome. There is a 7-day stay limit. Reservations are accepted and can be made online at recreation.gov or by calling 877-444-6777.

PARK DETAILS

Navajo National Monument

PO Box 7717
Shonto, AZ 86045
Phone: 928-672-2700

Description

Navajo National Monument preserves three cliff dwellings of the Ancestral Puebloan people. Rangers guide visitors on tours of the Keet Seel/Kawestima and Betatakin/Talastima cliff dwellings. The Sandal Trail (1.3 miles round trip) starts at the visitor center and leads to an overlook of the Betatakin/Talastima dwelling.

Information

Information is available from the visitor center at the end of SR-564 nine miles north of the Black Mesa Junction at US-160. Exhibits feature various artifacts from Anasazi and Navajo culture. A craft shop is also within the visitor center building. In summer, the visitor center is open daily from 8am to 5:30pm. The rest of the year it is open daily from 9am to 5pm.

Fees & Season

No entrance fee is charged. The park remains open year-round.

Directions

Navajo National Monument is in northeast Arizona about 135 miles north of Flagstaff. From Flagstaff, follow US-89 north for 62 miles then US-160 northeast for 63 miles and SR-564 north for nine miles.

RV CAMPING

Sunset View Campground

Located near the visitor center. Open all year, 31 small sites with picnic tables and charcoal grills, free, drinking water, restrooms with flush toilets. Open campfires are prohibited. Pets welcome. The campground can accommodate RVs up to 28 feet at some sites. Sites are available on a first-come, first-served basis; reservations are not accepted.

PARK DETAILS

Organ Pipe Cactus National Monument

10 Organ Pipe Dr
Ajo, AZ 85321
Phone: 520-387-6849

Description

Organ Pipe Cactus National Monument protects over 330,000 acres of southern Arizona's Sonoran Desert wildlife and landscape. The monument exhibits an extraordinary collection of plants, including the organ pipe cactus, a large cactus rarely found in the United States. More than 200,000 people visit the park each year.

Scenic Drives

A popular scenic drive within the park is the 21-mile Ajo Mountain Drive, which is a mostly gravel road usually passable in passenger cars. The road may become impassable during the summer monsoon season. RVs over 24 feet are prohibited. A free guidebook describing the tour is available from the visitor center.

Information

Information is available from the Kris Eggle Visitor Center located on SR-85 about 33 miles south of Ajo. The center is open daily from 8:30am to 4:30pm, excluding Thanksgiving and Christmas Day. The visitor center features a museum with photographic exhibits and dioramas on the Sonoran Desert.

Fees & Season

An entrance fee of $12 is charged and is valid for seven days. The park remains open year-round.

Directions

Organ Pipe Cactus National Monument lies in southern Arizona south of Ajo, which is about 130 miles west of Tucson via SR-86. Most of the park is accessed from SR-85.

RV CAMPING

Twin Peaks Campground

Located 1.5 miles south of the park's visitor center. Open all year, 174 sites with picnic tables and fire grates, $16 per night, drinking water, restrooms with flush toilets, solar showers, dump station. Pets welcome. The campground can accommodate RVs up to 45 feet at four sites. There is a 21-day stay limit. Reservations are required during the peak season (January through March) and can by made online at recreation.gov or by calling 877-444-6777.

PARK DETAILS

Sunset Crater Volcano National Monument

Flagstaff Area National Monuments
6400 US Highway 89
Flagstaff, AZ 86004
Phone: 928-526-0502

Description

Sunset Crater Volcano National Monument is in north-central Arizona, northeast of Flagstaff. The park's primary attraction is the large cinder cone rising 1,000 feet above the surrounding landscape. Visitors will also find pueblos and cliff dwellings in the area. The park receives nearly 200,000 visitors each year.

Information

Information is available from the visitor center located two miles east of US-89 on Sunset Crater Wupatki Loop Road. The visitor center is open daily all year from 9am to 5pm except on Christmas Day. Special programs are generally offered during summer months.

Fees & Season

An entrance fee of $25 is charged and is valid for seven days. The park remains open year-round.

Directions

From Flagstaff, follow US-89 north for 12 miles; turn east on Sunset Crater Wupatki Loop Rd and follow for two miles to the park's visitor center.

RV CAMPING

Bonito Campground

U.S. Forest Service campground located near the park's visitor center. Open May to early October, 44 sites with picnic tables and fire grates, $24 per night, drinking water, restrooms with flush toilets. Pets welcome. The campground can accommodate RVs up to 42 feet at some sites. There is a 14-day stay limit. Sites are available on a first-come, first-served basis; reservations are not accepted.

Arkansas

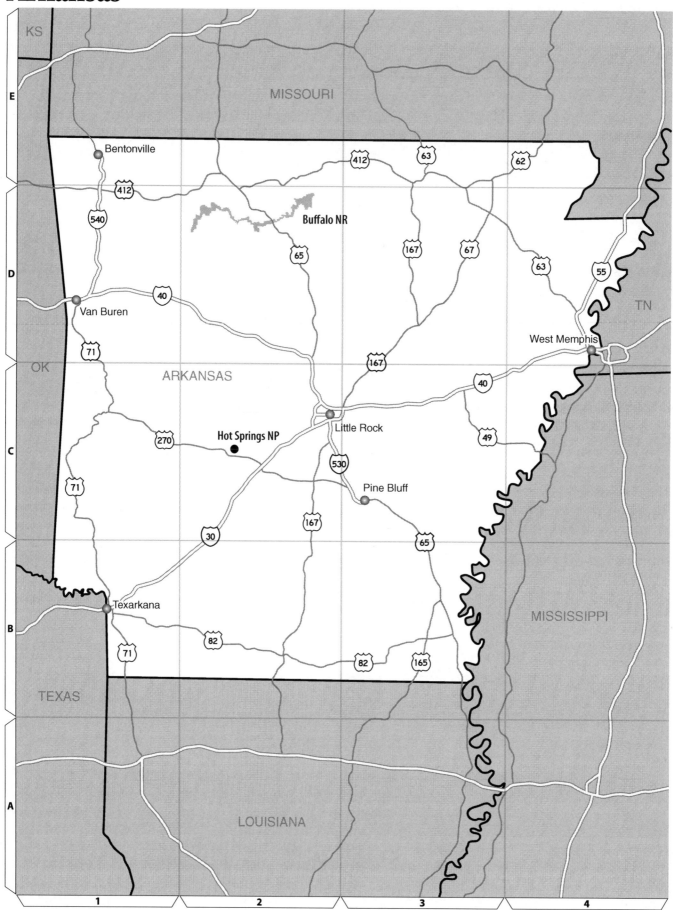

KS

MISSOURI

Bentonville

412

540

Buffalo NR

65

167

67

Van Buren

40

63

55

71

TN

OK

ARKANSAS

167

West Memphis

40

Hot Springs NP

Little Rock

270

49

530

C

Pine Bluff

71

167

30

65

Texarkana

MISSISSIPPI

82

71

82

165

TEXAS

LOUISIANA

Arkansas Parks

	Map	Auto Touring	Biking	Boating	Climbing	Fishing	Hiking	Horseback Riding	Hunting	Snow Skiing	Swimming	Visitor Center	Wildlife Viewing
Buffalo National River	D2	•		•		•	•	•	•		•	•	•
Hot Springs National Park	C2	•					•						•

PARK DETAILS

Buffalo National River

402 N Walnut, Suite 136
Harrison, AR 72601
Phone: 870-439-2502

Description

Buffalo National River preserves 135 miles of the 150-mile long river flowing across northern Arkansas. It begins as a trickle in the Boston Mountains 15 miles above the park boundary and meanders east through the Ozarks into the White River. Massive limestone bluffs contain the free-flowing river. More than one million people come to the park each year to float the river and enjoy the recreational opportunities.

Information

Information is available from the Tyler Bend Visitor Center, 12 miles north of Marshall off US-65. The visitor center is open all year except Thanksgiving Day, Christmas Day, and New Year's Day. Hours of operation are 8:30am to 4:30pm daily. Information is also available from the Buffalo Point Ranger Station and Steel Creek Information Station. Buffalo Point Ranger Station is open all year but closes on federal holidays except Memorial Day, Independence Day, and Labor Day. Hours of operation are 8:30am to 4:30pm daily as staffing permits. The Steel Creek Information Station is only open as staffing permits; call in advance to be certain the station is open (870-449-4311).

Fees & Season

No entrance fee is charged. The park remains open all year.

Directions

The park's headquarters is located in Harrison, Arkansas, along US-62. From there, visitors can reach the various districts by following state and federal highways. The Upper District is reached by following either SR-7 or SR-43. Areas within the Middle District are accessible off US-65. The Lower District is reached by following US-62 and SR-14.

RV CAMPING

Buffalo Point Campground

Located 17 miles southeast of Yellville on SR-268. Open mid-March to mid-September (Loop B remains open year-round but without services), 83 sites with hookups (30/50 amp), picnic tables and fire grates, $22 per night, drinking water, restrooms with flush toilets, showers, dump station. Pets welcome. The campground can accommodate large RVs over 40 feet at some sites. There is a 14-day stay limit. Reservations are accepted and can be made online at recreation.gov or by calling 877-444-6777.

Erbie Campground

Located about eight miles north of Jasper via SR-7 and CR-79/Erbie Campground Road. Access road is narrow in spots. Open year-round, 14 sites with picnic tables and fire grates, free, vault toilet. There are no hookups, no running water, and no dump station. Pets welcome. There is a 14-day stay limit. Sites are available on a first-come, first-served basis; reservations are not accepted.

Ozark Campground

Located six miles north of Jasper via SR-7 and CR-129. Open year-round, 31 sites with picnic tables and fire grates, $16 per night, drinking water (shut off in winter), restrooms with flush toilets, vault toilets in off-season. Pets welcome. There is a 14-day stay limit. Sites are available on a first-come, first-served basis; reservations are not accepted.

Tyler Bend Campground

Located 12 miles northwest of Marshall off US-65 via CR-241 and CR-231. Open all year, 28 sites with picnic tables and fire grates, $16 per night, drinking water, restrooms with flush toilets, showers, dump station. Pets welcome. The campground can accommodate RVs up to 28 feet at some sites. There is a 14-day stay limit. Sites are available on a first-come, first-served basis; reservations are not accepted.

PARK DETAILS

Hot Springs National Park

101 Reserve St
Hot Springs, AR 71901
Phone: 501-620-6715

Description

Hot Springs National Park is in central Arkansas about 50 miles southwest of Little Rock. The park was first established as Hot Springs Reservation on April 20, 1832 to protect hot springs flowing from the southwestern slope of Hot Springs Mountain. The park protects eight historic bathhouses, contains about 5,500 acres and attracts more than one million visitors annually. The historic bathhouses are located along Bathhouse Row on Central Ave (SR-7) in downtown Hot Springs.

Information

Information is available from the visitor center located in the former Fordyce Bathhouse on Bathhouse Row in downtown Hot Springs. Bathhouse Row is on Central Avenue between Reserve and Fountain Streets. The visitor center is open 9am to 5pm year-round except Thanksgiving, Christmas, and New Year's Day.

Fees & Season

There is no entrance fee. Fees are charged if staying overnight in the campground or visiting the Hot Springs Mountain Tower. The park remains open year-round.

Directions

Hot Springs National Park is about 18 miles off I-30 in downtown Hot Springs; Bathhouse Row is on Central Avenue. Interstate 30 travelers can take Exit 98B and follow US-270 into Hot Springs.

RV CAMPING

Gulpha Gorge Campground

Located off US-70B on the east side of Hot Springs. Open year-round, 44 sites with picnic tables and grills, drinking water, restrooms with flush toilets, dump station, no showers. All sites include 30 and 50 amp electric hookups, water, and sewer connections. Cost is $30 per night. Pets welcome. The campground can accommodate large RVs at most sites. There is a 14 day stay limit. Sites are available on a first-come, first-served basis; reservations are not accepted.

California

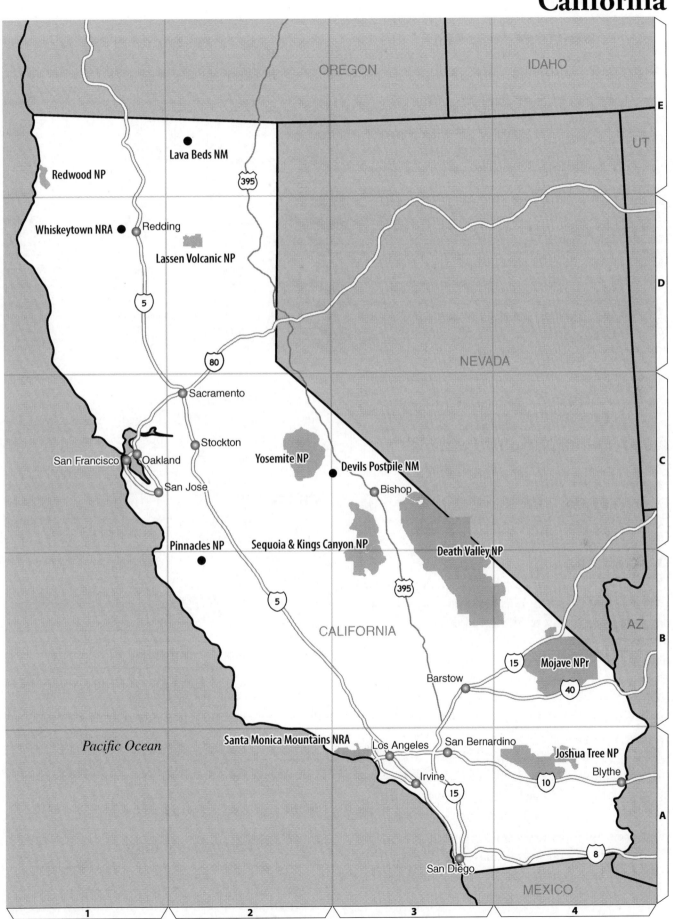

OREGON

IDAHO

UT

Lava Beds NM

Redwood NP

Whiskeytown NRA ● Redding

Lassen Volcanic NP

NEVADA

Sacramento

Stockton

San Francisco ○ Oakland

San Jose

Yosemite NP

Devils Postpile NM

Bishop

Pinnacles NP

Sequoia & Kings Canyon NP

Death Valley NP

CALIFORNIA

AZ

Mojave NPr

Barstow

Pacific Ocean

Santa Monica Mountains NRA

Los Angeles

San Bernardino

Joshua Tree NP

Irvine

Blythe

San Diego

MEXICO

California Parks

California Parks	Map	Auto Touring	Biking	Boating	Climbing	Fishing	Hiking	Horseback Riding	Hunting	Snow Skiing	Swimming	Visitor Center	Wildlife Viewing
Death Valley National Park	B3	•	•				•	•			•	•	•
Devils Postpile National Monument	C3					•	•	•					•
Joshua Tree National Park	A4	•	•		•		•	•				•	
Lassen Volcanic National Park	D2	•	•	•		•	•	•		•	•	•	•
Lava Beds National Monument	E2	•	•				•	•				•	•
Mojave National Preserve	B4	•	•		•		•	•	•			•	•
Pinnacles National Park	B2				•		•					•	•
Redwood National Park	E1	•	•	•			•	•	•			•	•
Santa Monica Mountains National Recreation Area	A3	•	•			•	•	•			•	•	•
Sequoia & Kings Canyon National Parks	B3	•					•	•	•		•		•
Whiskeytown National Recreation Area	D1	•	•	•			•	•	•	•	•	•	•
Yosemite National Park	C2	•	•		•	•	•	•	•	•	•	•	•

PARK DETAILS

Death Valley National Park

PO Box 579
Death Valley, CA 92328
Phone: 760-786-3200

Description

Death Valley National Park in southern California contains more than 3.3 million acres of spectacular desert scenery. It features the lowest point in the western hemisphere; Badwater is 282 feet below sea level. The park is one of few designated an International Dark-Sky Park. More than one million visitors come to this park each year.

Information

Information is available from two visitor centers within the park. Furnace Creek Visitor Center remains open all year and is located along SR-190. Hours are 8am to 5pm. The visitor center features a 20-minute film about the park, which is shown throughout the day. Scotty's Castle Visitor Center is currently closed until further notice due to extensive flash flooding that occurred in October of 2015.

Fees & Season

An entrance fee of $30 is charged that is valid for seven days. The park remains open year-round and is most visited during winter.

Directions

Furnace Creek is in the heart of Death Valley National Park. The village is located along SR-190 approximately 120 miles northeast of Ridgecrest, California, or 60 miles west of Pahrump, Nevada.

RV CAMPING

Furnace Creek Campground

Located along SR-190 about 53 miles east of Panamint Springs. Open all year, 136 sites (some with hookups), picnic tables, fire pits, drinking water, flush toilets, dump station. Cost is $22 per night for a standard site and $36 for sites with hookups. There is a stay limit of 14 days and a 35-foot RV length limit. Reservations are accepted mid-October to mid-April and can be made online at recreation.gov or by calling 877-444-6777.

Mesquite Spring Campground

Located three miles south of Scotty's Castle off Scotty's Castle Road. Open year-round, 30 sites with picnic tables and fire pits, $14 per night, drinking water, flush toilets, dump station. There is a 30-day stay limit and a 35-foot RV length limit. Sites are available on a first-come, first-served basis; reservations are not accepted.

Stovepipe Wells Campground

Located in Stovepipe Wells Village along SR-190. Open mid-September to mid-May, 190 sites (some with picnic tables and fire rings), $14 per night, drinking water, restrooms with flush toilets, dump station. There is a 30-day stay limit and a 35-foot RV length limit. Sites are available on a first-come, first-served basis; reservations are not accepted.

Sunset Campground

Located in Furnace Creek off SR-190. Open November to mid-April, 270 sites, $14 per night, drinking water, restrooms with flush toilets, dump station. There is a 30-day stay limit and a 40-foot RV length limit. Sites are available on a first-come, first-served basis; reservations are not accepted.

Texas Spring Campground

Located in Furnace Creek off SR-190. Open mid-November to mid-April, 92 sites with tables and fire pits, $16 per night, drinking water, flush toilets, dump station. There is a 30-day stay limit and a 35-foot RV length limit. Sites are available on a first-come, first-served basis; reservations are not accepted.

Wildrose Campground

Located in the Panamint Mountains off Emmigrant Canyon Road. Open all year, 23 sites with tables and fire pits, free, drinking water, pit toilets. Drinking water not available in winter. There is a 30-day stay limit. Campground is not accessible to vehicles longer than 25 feet. Sites are available on a first-come, first-served basis; reservations are not accepted.

PARK DETAILS

Devils Postpile National Monument

PO Box 3999
Mammoth Lakes, CA 93546
Phone: 760-934-2289

Description

Devils Postpile National Monument protects the unusual geologic formation known as "the Postpile," the 101-foot high Rainbow Falls, and surrounding mountains. Nearly 75 percent of the 800-acre monument is preserved as part of the Ansel Adams Wilderness. The John Muir and Pacific Crest Trails can be accessed within the monument. Inyo National Forest surrounds the monument. Most park visitors are required to ride a shuttle bus into the park, however, visitors staying in the park's campground are excepted.

Information

Information is available from the Devils Postpile Ranger Station located just inside the monument's entrance. The ranger station is usually open summer to early fall.

Fees & Season

Devils Postpile is typically open and accessible from mid-June to mid-October but most visitors come in July and August. A one-day pass to ride the shuttle bus costs $8 per person. If staying in the campground, the cost of a camping pass is $10 and is good for the duration of stay. The pass fee is in addition to camping fees.

Directions

Devils Postpile National Monument is in central California about 50 miles northwest of Bishop via US-395 and SR-203.

RV CAMPING

Devils Postpile Campground

Located near the ranger station. Open July to mid-September depending on weather, 20 sites with picnic tables and fire grates, $20 per night, drinking water, restrooms with flush toilets. Bear-resistant lockers provided at each site. Pets welcome. The campground can accommodate RVs up to 30 feet at some sites; most site lengths range between 20 and 25 feet. There is a 14-day stay limit. Sites are available on a first-come, first-served basis; reservations are not accepted. **NOTE:** At present, the campground is closed until further notice.

PARK DETAILS

Joshua Tree National Park

74485 National Park Dr
Twentynine Palms, CA 92277
Phone: 760-367-5500

Description

Two deserts come together at Joshua Tree National Park. The Colorado Desert lies within the eastern part of the park and features natural gardens of creosote bush, ocotillo, and cholla cactus. The higher, moister, and slightly cooler Mojave Desert in the western part of the park is where you'll find Joshua trees. The park is one of few designated an International Dark-Sky Park.

Information

Information is available from three visitor centers. Cottonwood Visitor Center is located in the southern part of the park about seven miles north of Interstate 10 Exit 168. The visitor center is open all year, 8:30am to 4pm daily. Joshua Tree Visitor Center is one block south of SR-62 at Park Boulevard in Joshua Tree. The visitor center is open daily all year from 8am to 5pm. Oasis Visitor Center is located at the park's headquarters in Twentynine Palms, California, at the junction of Utah Trail and National Park Drive. The center is open all year, 8:30am to 5pm daily.

Fees & Season

An entrance fee of $30 is charged and is good for seven days. The park remains open all year; visitation increases as temperatures moderate in the fall and peaks during the spring wildflower season.

Directions

Joshua Tree National Park lies in southeast California. There are three primary entrance points; two on the northern side of the park, one on the south. The southern entrance is off Interstate 10 at Exit 168. One of the northern entrances is near Joshua Tree along Park Boulevard and the other is near Twentynine Palms on Utah Trail.

RV CAMPING

Belle Campground

Located about ten miles south of Twentynine Palms on Utah Trail. Open October through May, 18 sites with picnic tables and fire grates, $15 per night, no water, pit toilets. Pets welcome. There is a 14-day stay limit. The campground can accommodate RVs up to 35 feet at some sites. Sites are available on a first-come, first-served basis; reservations are not accepted.

Black Rock Campground

Located south of Yucca Valley on Joshua Lane. Open all year, 99 sites with picnic tables and fire grates, $20 per night, drinking water, restrooms with flush toilets, dump station. Pets welcome. The campground can accommodate RVs up to 42 feet at some sites. There is a 14-day stay limit October through May (30 days other months). Reservations are accepted and can be made online at recreation.gov or by calling 877-444-6777. A designated horse camp area is also available for $20 per night.

Cottonwood Campground

Located on Cottonwood Spring Road about seven miles north of I-10. Open year-round, 62 sites with picnic tables and fire grates, $20 per night, drinking water, restrooms with flush toilets, dump station. Pets welcome. The campground can accommodate RVs up to 35 feet at some sites. There is a 14-day stay limit October through May (30 days other months). Reservations are accepted and can be made online at recreation.gov or by calling 877-444-6777.

Hidden Valley Campground

Located 14 miles southeast of Joshua Tree along Park Boulevard. Open year-round, 44 sites with picnic tables and fire grates, $15 per night, no drinking water, pit toilets. Pets welcome. RVs and trailers may not exceed a combined maximum length of 25 feet. There is a 14-day stay limit October through May (30 days other months). Sites are available on a first-come, first-served basis; reservations are not accepted.

Indian Cove Campground

Located about five miles west of Twentynine Palms and three miles south of CA 62 on Indian Cove Road. Open year-round, 101 sites with picnic tables and fire grates, $20 per night, no drinking water, pit toilets. Pets welcome. Drinking water is available at the nearby ranger station. The campground can accommodate RVs up to 35 feet at some sites. There is a 14-day stay limit October through May (30 days other months). Reservations are accepted and can be made online at recreation.gov or by calling 877-444-6777.

Jumbo Rocks Campground

Located 11 miles south of Twentynine Palms along Park Boulevard. Open year-round, 124 sites with picnic tables and fire grates, $15 per night, no drinking water, pit toilets. Pets welcome. The campground can accommodate RVs up to 35 feet at some sites. There is a 14-day stay limit October through May (30 days other months). Reservations are accepted and can be made online at recreation.gov or by calling 877-444-6777.

Ryan Campground

Located 16 miles southeast of Joshua Tree off Park Boulevard. Open October through May, 31 sites with picnic tables and fire grates, $15 per night, no drinking water, pit toilets. Pets welcome. There is a 14-day stay limit. Sites are available on a first-come, first-served basis; reservations are not accepted. A designated horse camp area also is available for $15 per night. Reservations are required for sites in the horse camp area and can be made online at recreation.gov or by calling 877-444-6777.

White Tank Campground

Located 11 miles south of Twentynine Palms. Open October through May, 15 sites with picnic tables and fire grates, $15 per night, no drinking water, pit toilets. Pets welcome. RVs and trailers may not exceed a combined maximum length of 25 feet. There is a 14-day stay limit. Sites are available on a first-come, first-served basis; reservations are not accepted.

PARK DETAILS

Lassen Volcanic National Park

PO Box 100
Mineral, CA 96063
Phone: 530-595-4480

Description

Lassen Volcanic National Park protects over 106,000 acres of mountain meadows and lakes, fumaroles, and numerous volcanoes. All four types of volcanoes in the world can be found in the park, which receives around 350,000 visitors each year.

Information

Information is available from the Kohm Yah-mah-nee Visitor Center near the southwest entrance on SR-89. The visitor center is open daily from 9am to 5pm, May through October. It is open Wednesday through Sunday, November through April (except Thanksgiving and Christmas Day). A cafe and gift shop is also located inside the visitor center. Information is also available from the Loomis Museum at the northwest park entrance on SR-89. The museum is open late May through October.

Fees & Season

Lassen Volcanic National Park remains open year-round but access may be limited during winter months. An entrance fee of $25 is charged and is valid for seven days.

Directions

The northwestern entrance to the park is approximately 50 miles east of Redding, California, via SR-44. The southwest entrance is about 50 miles east of Red Bluff, California, via SR-36 and SR-89.

RV CAMPING

Butte Lake Campground

Located about 17 miles from Old Station and six miles south of SR-44 via Butte Lake Rd. Open June through October (weather permitting), 101 sites with picnic tables and fire grates, $22 per night, drinking water, vault toilets. Pets welcome. The campground can accommodate RVs up to 35 feet at some sites. There is a 14-day stay limit. Reservations are accepted and can be made online at recreation.gov or by calling 877-444-6777.

Manzanita Lake Campground

Located adjacent to Manzanita Lake off SR-89. Open late May until snow closure (usually late October), 179 sites with picnic tables and fire grates, some pull-through sites, $26 per night, drinking water, flush and vault toilets, dump station, showers, laundry, food, gift shop, boat launch. Pets welcome. The campground can accommodate RVs up to 40 feet at some sites. There is a 14-day stay limit. Reservations are accepted and can be made online at recreation.gov or by calling 877-444-6777. The Manzanita Lake Camper Store carries apparel, gifts, groceries, beverages, sundries, ice, firewood, fishing tackle, camping equipment, and basic automotive supplies. Fuel, pay phone, and ATM are also available.

Summit Lake North Campground

Located off SR-89 about 12 miles southeast of Manzanita Lake. Open late June through September (weather permitting), 46 sites with picnic tables and fire grates, some pull-thrus, $24 per night, drinking water, restrooms with flush toilets. Pets welcome. The campground can accommodate RVs up to 35 feet at some sites. There is a 7-day stay limit. Reservations are accepted and can be made online at recreation.gov or by calling 877-444-6777.

PARK DETAILS

Lava Beds National Monument

PO Box 1240
Tulelake, CA 96134
Phone: 530-667-8113

Description

Lava Beds National Monument contains 46,500 acres of cinder cones, lava flows, and numerous lava tube caves. There are over 20 developed caves that park visitors may wish to explore. Most caves are open for exploration without a guide and many are well marked and easily accessible. Crystal Ice Cave is only open to visitors on small ranger-guided tours once a week during winter. Fern Cave is open to visitors on ranger-guided tours once a week during the summer months.

Information

Information is available from the visitor center located along the park road in the southern part of the monument. The visitor center is open daily all year except December 25th. Summer hours are 9am to 5:30pm. Fall and spring hours are 9am to 4:30pm. Winter hours are 10am to 4pm.

Fees & Season

An entrance fee of $25 is charged. The park remains open year-round but snow can temporarily close park roads until they are plowed.

Directions

Lava Beds National Monument is in northeast California about 70 miles northwest of Alturas via SR-299 and SR-139.

RV CAMPING

Indian Well Campground

Located at the south end of the park near the visitor center. Open all year, 43 sites with picnic tables and fire grates, $10 per night, drinking water, restrooms with flush toilets. Pets welcome. The campground can accommodate RVs up to 30 feet at some sites. There is a 14-day stay limit. Sites are available on a first-come, first-served basis; reservations are not accepted. Note that the monument is unable to accept debit or credit cards for campground fees; only cash or checks are accepted.

PARK DETAILS

Mojave National Preserve

2701 Barstow Rd
Barstow, CA 92311
Phone: 760-252-6100

Description

Mojave National Preserve protects 1.6 million acres of sand dunes, volcanic cinder cones, and Joshua tree forests within its canyons, mountains, and mesas. The park is the third largest unit of the National Park System in the contiguous United States. More than 500,000 visitors come to the park each year.

Information

Information is available from the park's headquarters in Barstow; a park ranger is on duty to help with trip planning. Within the park, information is available at the Kelso Depot Visitor Center, which is about 22 miles north of I-40 via Kelbaker Rd. It is typically open Thursday through Monday from 10am to 5pm (except Christmas Day). Information is also available at the Hole-in-the-Wall Information Center, located 20 miles north of I-40 via Essex and Black Canyon Roads.

Fees & Season

The park is open year-round. No entrance fee is charged.

Directions

The vast park lies between Interstates 15 and 40, east of Barstow. The Kelso Depot Visitor Center can be reached from I-15 by exiting at Kelbaker Road in Baker and driving south for 34 miles. From I-40, the visitor center is reached by exiting at Kelbaker Road and driving north for 22 miles.

RV CAMPING

Hole-in-the-Wall Campground

Located ten miles north of I-40 via Essex Road and Black Canyon Road. Open all year, 35 sites with picnic tables and fire grates, $12 per night, drinking water, vault toilets, dump station. Pets welcome. Sites are available on a first-come, first-served basis; reservations are not accepted.

PARK DETAILS

Pinnacles National Park

5000 Hwy 146
Paicines, CA 95043
Phone: 831-389-4486

Description

Pinnacles National Park preserves 26,425 acres of rocky spires and crags surrounded by rolling hills and mountains. The park is primarily a hiking park as there are numerous trails leading to overlooks and talus caves. There are two entrances into the park but no through-road. The eastern entrance provides access to most of the park's amenities and facilities, including the campground. The western entrance is primarily used by visitors interested in accessing hiking trails in the Chaparral area. The access road to the western portion of the monument is steep and narrow; RVs are not recommended. The park experiences extremely high visitation on weekends and holidays, especially in March and April.

Information

Information is available from the Pinnacles Visitor Center in the eastern portion of the park along SR-146. The visitor center is open daily from 9:30am to 5pm. Information is also available from the West Pinnacles Visitor Contact Station, which is open daily from 9am to 4:30pm.

Fees & Season

The east entrance to the park is open 24 hours a day, seven days a week. A gate to the park's west entrance opens at 7:30am and closes at 8pm. An entrance fee of $30 is charged and is valid for seven days.

Directions

From the San Francisco Bay area to the east entrance, follow US-101 south through the city of Gilroy to SR-25. Follow SR-25 south about 40 miles to SR-146, which will lead you to the Pinnacles Visitor Center and campground area.

RV CAMPING

Pinnacles Campground

Located in the eastern portion of the park along SR-146 about two miles south of SR-25. Open all year, 36 sites with electric hookups ($36 per night), 82 standard sites ($23 per night), shared picnic tables and barbecue grills, drinking water, restrooms with flush toilets, showers (fee charged), dump station, swimming pool. Pets welcome. The campground can accommodate large RVs at most sites. Campfires permitted only when fire danger conditions are low. A general store with basic foods and camping supplies is located on-site. Reservations are accepted and can be made online at recreation.gov or by calling 877-444-6777.

PARK DETAILS

Redwood National and State Parks

1111 Second St
Crescent City, CA 95531
Phone: 707-465-7335

Description

Redwood National and State Parks preserve 133,000 acres of forests, prairies, oak woodlands, wild riverways, and nearly 40 miles of coastline. The area is a cooperative management effort between the National Park Service and California Department of Parks and Recreation. Thirty-five percent of all the old-growth redwood forest remaining in California is contained within the federal unit and three state parks.

Scenic Drives

Newton B. Drury Scenic Parkway is a ten-mile paved route suitable for all types of vehicles. The scenic drive passes through the heart of the old-growth redwood forest in Prairie Creek Redwoods State Park and is an alternative to US-101. There are several other scenic drives within the parks but RVs are prohibited or not advised to travel.

Information

Information is available from three visitor centers and two information centers. Jedediah Smith Visitor Center is on US-199 at the Jedediah Smith Campground and is open only in summer. Prairie Creek Visitor Center is just off US-101 along Newton B. Drury Scenic Parkway and is open all year except New Year's Day, Thanksgiving Day, and Christmas Day. The Thomas H. Kuchel Visitor Center is along US-101 at Orick and is open year-round except New Year's Day, Thanksgiving Day, and Christmas Day. Crescent City Information Center is at 1111 Second Street in Crescent City and is open daily all year except New Year's Day, Thanksgiving Day, and Christmas Day. The Hiouchi Information Center is open daily in summer and is located along US-199 at Hiouchi.

Fees & Season

The parks remain open all year. No entrance fee is charged in the National Park Service unit. Day-use fees are collected in the various state park units.

Directions

Redwood National and State Parks is generally oriented north-south along the US-101 highway corridor in northwest California between Crescent City and Orick.

RV CAMPING

Elk Prairie Campground

Located on Newton B. Drury Scenic Parkway in Prairie Creek Redwoods State Park. Open all year, 75 sites with picnic tables and fire grates, $35 per night, drinking water, restrooms with flush toilets, showers. Pets welcome. The campground can accommodate motor homes up to 27 feet and trailers up to 24 feet at some sites. There is a 14-day stay limit. Reservations are accepted and can be made online at reservecalifornia.com or by calling 800-444-7275.

Gold Bluffs Beach Campground

Located in Prairie Creek Redwoods State Park ten miles north of Orick on unpaved Davison Road. Open April to September, 26 sites with picnic tables and fire grates, $35 per night, drinking water, restrooms with flush toilets, solar showers. Pets welcome. The campground can accommodate motor homes up to 24 feet long and 8 feet wide (trailers prohibited). There is a 14-day stay limit. Sites are available on a first-come, first-served basis; reservations are not accepted.

Jedediah Smith Campground

Located nine miles east of Crescent City along US-199 in Jedediah Smith Redwoods State Park. Open all year, 86 sites with picnic tables and fire grates, $35 per night, drinking water, restrooms with flush toilets, showers, dump station. Pets welcome. The campground can accommodate motor homes up to 25 feet long and trailers up to 21 feet long. There is a 14-day stay limit. Reservations are accepted and can be made online at reservecalifornia.com or by calling 800-444-7275.

Mill Creek Campground

Located seven miles south of Crescent City off US-101 in Del Norte Coast Redwoods State Park. Open May to September, 145 sites with picnic tables and fire grates, $35 per night, drinking water, restrooms with flush toilets, showers, dump station. The campground can accommodate motor homes up to 28 feet long and trailers up to 24 feet long. There is a 14-day stay limit. Reservations are accepted and can be made online at reservecalifornia.com or by calling 800-444-7275.

PARK DETAILS

Santa Monica Mountains National Recreation Area

26876 Mulholland Hwy
Calabasas, CA 91302
Phone: 805-370-2301

Description

The Santa Monica Mountains National Recreation Area encompasses 150,000 acres of mountains, canyons, woodlands, and miles of beaches. It was established in 1978 and is managed cooperatively by federal, state, and local park agencies. More than 500 miles of trails are available for hikers, runners, mountain bikers, and equestrians.

Information

Information is available from the Anthony C. Beilenson Interagency Visitor Center at King Gillette Ranch, which is located at 26876 Mulholland Highway in Calabasas. The visitor center is operated by four partner agencies.

Fees & Season

The recreation area is open year-round. No entrance fee is charged.

Directions

The recreation area lies just to the northwest of Los Angeles and is accessible from several locations along US-101 and SR-1. The area's information center can be reached from US-101 by following Las Virgenes Rd south about four miles and then going east on Mulholland Highway for one-tenth of a mile.

RV CAMPING

There are four camping areas within the recreation area and all are managed by the State of California. Please note that federal discount passes may not be honored in California state parks.

Canyon Campground

Located in Leo Carrillo State Park on the Pacific Coast Highway about 28 miles northwest of Santa Monica. Open all year, 90 non-electric sites ($45 per night), 50 sites with electric ($60 per night), picnic table and fire ring at each site, drinking water, flush toilets, showers, dump station. There is a seven-day stay limit in summer. The campground can accommodate RVs up to 31 feet long. Reservations are accepted and can be made online at reservecalifornia.com or by calling 800-444-7275.

Malibu Creek Campground

Located in Malibu Creek State Park, four miles south of US-101 on Las Virgenes Rd. Open all year, 63 sites with tables and fire rings, $45 per night, drinking water, flush toilets, showers, dump station, laundry. There is a seven-day stay limit in summer. The campground can accommodate RVs up to 30 feet long. Reservations are accepted and can be made online at reservecalifornia.com or by calling 800-444-7275.

Sycamore Canyon Campground

Located in Point Mugu State Park on the Pacific Coast Highway about 32 miles northwest of Santa Monica. Open all year, 58 sites with tables and fire rings, $45 per night, drinking water, flush toilets, showers, dump station. There is a seven-day stay limit in summer. The campground can accommodate RVs up to 31 feet long. Reservations are accepted and can be made online at reservecalifornia.com or by calling 800-444-7275.

Thornhill Broome Campground

Located in Point Mugu State Park on the Pacific Coast Highway about 34 miles northwest of Santa Monica. Open all year, 64 sites with tables and fire rings, $35 per night, drinking water, chemical toilets. There is a seven-day stay limit in summer. The campground can accommodate RVs up to 31 feet long. Reservations are accepted and can be made online at reservecalifornia.com or by calling 800-444-7275.

PARK DETAILS

Sequoia & Kings Canyon National Parks

47050 Generals Highway
Three Rivers, CA 93271
Phone: 559-565-3341

Description

Sequoia and Kings Canyon National Parks are two separate parks managed as one. Together, the parks preserve immense mountains, deep canyons, and towering sequoia trees. Sequoia National Park contains the tallest mountain in the lower 48 states, 14,494-foot Mount Whitney. Kings Canyon National Park is home to North America's deepest canyon.

Information

Information is available from four visitor centers. Foothills Visitor Center and Lodgepole Visitor Center are located within Sequoia National Park. The first is on Generals Highway about one mile from the Ash Mountain Entrance. It is open daily year-round between 8am and 4:30pm. The latter is on Lodgepole Road about 21 miles north of the Ash Mountain Entrance. It is open seasonally. Kings Canyon Visitor Center in Grant Grove is about three miles east of the Big Stump Entrance on SR-180. It is open daily all year from 9am to 5pm (9am to 4pm in winter). Cedar Grove Visitor Center is on SR-180 about 30 miles east of Grant Grove. It closes in winter but is otherwise open daily from 9am to 5pm.

Fees & Season

The parks remain open year-round; highest visitation is in July and August. Occasional winter storms may close roads leading into the parks until they can be plowed. An entrance fee of $35 is charged that is valid for seven days.

Directions

Two state highways enter the parks. California Highway 180 east from Fresno enters the Grant Grove area of Kings Canyon National Park and continues 30 miles to the Cedar Grove area. California Highway 198 enters Sequoia National Park about 35 miles east of Visalia. Inside the parks' boundaries both become the Generals Highway, often referred to as "the road between the parks."

RV CAMPING

The following campgrounds are located within Kings Canyon National Park.

Azalea Campground

Located in the Grant Grove area 3.5 miles from the park entrance. Open all year, 110 sites with tables and fire rings, $18 per night, drinking water, flush toilets. Groceries and laundry facilities are in nearby Grant Grove Village. Pets welcome. There is a 14 day stay limit in summer. Sites are only available on a first-come, first-served basis.

Crystal Springs Campground

Located 4 miles from the park entrance in the Grant Grove area. Open mid-May to early September, 36 sites with tables and fire rings, $18 per night, drinking water, flush toilets. Groceries and laundry facilities are in nearby Grant Grove Village. Pets welcome. There is a 14 day stay limit in summer. Sites are only available on a first-come, first-served basis.

Moraine Campground

Located on SR-180 in the canyon near the Middle Fork of the Kings River about 3/4 mile from Cedar Grove Village. Open mid-May to early September, 121 sites with tables and fire rings, $18 per night, drinking water, flush toilets. Groceries, showers, and laundry facilities are nearby in Cedar Grove Village. Pets welcome. There is a 14 day stay limit in summer. Sites are only available on a first-come, first-served basis.

Sentinel Campground

Located 1/4 mile from Cedar Grove Village on SR-180. The campground is situated in the canyon along the South Fork of the Kings River. Open late April to early November, 82 sites with tables and fire rings, $22 per night, drinking water, flush toilets. Groceries, showers, and laundry facilities are nearby in Cedar Grove Village. Pets welcome. There is a 14 day stay limit in summer. Reservations are accepted and can be made online at recreation.gov or by calling 877-444-6777.

Sheep Creek Campground

Located on SR-180 about 1/4 mile from Cedar Grove Village. The campground is situated in the canyon near the Middle Fork of the Kings River. Open mid-May to mid-September, 111 sites with tables and fire rings, $18 per night, drinking water, flush toilets. Groceries, showers, and laundry facilities are in nearby Cedar Grove Village. Pets welcome. There is a 14 day stay limit in summer. Sites are available on a first-come, first-served basis; reservations are not accepted.

Sunset Campground

Located in the Grant Grove area about 3 miles from the park entrance. Open mid-May to early September, 157 sites with tables and fire rings, $22 per night, drinking water, flush toilets. Groceries and laundry facilities are in nearby Grant Grove Village. Pets welcome. There is a 14 day stay limit in summer. Reservations are accepted and can be made online at recreation.gov or by calling 877-444-6777.

The following campgrounds are located within Sequoia National Park.

Dorst Creek Campground

Located 12 miles north of Giant Forest on Generals Highway. Open mid-June to late September, 218 sites with tables and fire rings, $22 per night, drinking water, flush toilets, dump station. Pets welcome. There is a 14 day maximum stay limit. Reservations are accepted and can be made online at recreation.gov or by calling 877-444-6777.

Lodgepole Campground

Located off Generals Highway two miles north of Giant Forest and 21 miles from park entrance. Open April to November, 214 sites with tables and fire rings, $22 per night, drinking water, flush toilets, dump station. Restaurant, market, gift shop, laundry, and showers nearby. There is a 14 day maximum stay limit. Reservations are accepted and can be made online at recreation.gov or by calling 877-444-6777.

Potwisha Campground

Located four miles from the park entrance along SR-198. Open all year, 42 sites with tables and fire rings, $22 per night, drinking water, flush toilets, dump station. Pets welcome. There is a 14 day maximum stay limit in summer. Reservations are accepted and can be made online at recreation.gov or by calling 877-444-6777.

PARK DETAILS

Whiskeytown National Recreation Area

PO Box 188
Whiskeytown, CA 96095
Phone: 530-242-3400

Description

Whiskeytown National Recreation Area was established in 1972 and contains over 42,000 acres. The park features a 3,200-acre reservoir surrounded by mountainous back country. Also within the recreation area are four waterfalls and remains of structures built during the Gold Rush. Nearly 800,000 people visit each year to enjoy the park's outdoor recreation opportunities.

Information

Information is available from the Whiskeytown Visitor Center located along CA 299 at J. F. Kennedy Memorial

Drive, about eight miles west of Redding. The center is open daily except Thanksgiving, Christmas and New Years Day. Hours are 10am to 4pm. Exhibits depicting the California Gold Rush and a wide selection of books are among the center's features.

Fees & Season

The park is typically accessible year-round. An entrance fee of $25 is charged and is valid for seven days.

Directions

The park is located in northern California about eight miles west of Redding along SR-299.

RV CAMPING

Brandy Creek RV Campground

Located five miles off SR-299 along Kennedy Drive. Open year-round, 32 sites, $15 per night, water, dump station, public phone. There are no hookups or restrooms. There is a 14-day maximum stay limit. The campground can accommodate RVs up to 35 feet long. Sites are available on a first-come, first-served basis (reservations not accepted) and are paved parking spots on an access road.

Oak Bottom Campground

Concessionaire campground located 13 miles west of Redding on SR-299. Open all year, 22 sites, $21 per night from mid-April to mid-October, $14 per night from mid-October to mid-April, restrooms, showers, dump station. A swim beach is nearby. The RV sites do not have tables, hookups, or fire grates. Pets are allowed for a fee ($2 per pet, per day). Federal discount passes are honored and provide a 50 percent discount off camping fees. From mid-May through mid-September, the length of stay limit is 14 days. From mid-September to mid-May, the length of stay limit is 30 days. Reservations are accepted and can be made by calling the campground store at 530-359-2269.

PARK DETAILS

Yosemite National Park

PO Box 577
Yosemite, CA 95389
Phone: 209-372-0200

Description

Yosemite National Park encompasses 748,000 acres of beautiful mountain and valley scenery in the Sierra Nevada Mountains. Established in 1890, it is probably best known for its waterfalls but the park also features deep valleys, grand meadows, giant sequoias, a vast wilderness area, and more. Visitation is highest from May through October when nearly three million people come to the park.

Scenic Drives

Tioga Road is a 39-mile scenic drive from Crane Flat to Tioga Pass. The road is typically open from late May/early June to November. The route follows SR-120, a two-lane paved road suitable for all types of vehicles.

Information

Information is available from three visitor centers. Tuolumne Meadows Visitor Center is located in the eastern portion of the park along Tioga Road. It is only open daily in summer between 9am and 6pm. The Yosemite Valley Visitor Center is open year-round from 9am to 5pm. In addition to information, maps, and books, two films are shown daily every half hour. The Wawona Visitor Center is open daily from 8:30am to 5pm. It is located on the grounds of the Big Trees Lodge and offers information about park activities, wilderness permits, trail information, books, bear canister rentals, and maps. Information may also be obtained from the Big Oak Flat Information Station located just inside the park's western entrance on SR-120.

Fees & Season

An entrance fee of $35 per vehicle is charged. The park remains open year-round but some roads are closed due to snow from November through May.

Directions

Yosemite National Park is located in east-central California. It can be accessed year-round from the west by following SR-120 from Manteca or SR-120 from Merced. From Fresno and points south, visitors can enter the park's south entrance by following SR-41 north out of Fresno. In summer, the park can be accessed from the east by following SR-120 out of Lee Vining on US-395.

RV CAMPING

Bridalveil Creek Campground

Located off Glacier Point Road about eight miles east of its intersection with Wawona Road. Open July to late September, 110 sites, $18 per night, water, flush toilets. Equestrian sites available. None of the sites have RV hookups. Pets permitted. There is a 14-day stay limit. The campground can accommodate motor homes up to 35 feet and trailers up to 24 feet. Sites are available on a first-come, first-served basis; reservations are not accepted.

Crane Flat Campground

Located on Big Oak Flat Road (SR-120) just west of Crane Flat, about 15 miles west of Yosemite Valley. Open July through mid-October, 166 sites with picnic tables and fire rings, $26 per night, drinking water, flush toilets. None of the sites have RV hookups. Pets permitted. Camping is limited to 14 consecutive days. The campground can accommodate motor homes up to 35 feet and trailers up to 27 feet. Reservations are required and available online (recreation.gov) or by calling 877-444-6777 up to five months in advance.

Hodgdon Meadow Campground

Located adjacent to the Big Oak Flat Entrance Station on SR-120. Open all year, 105 sites with picnic tables and fire rings, $26 per night during peak season, $18 off season (mid-October to mid-April), drinking water, flush toilets. None of the sites have RV hookups. Pets permitted. Camping is limited to 14 consecutive days. The campground can accommodate motor homes up to 35 feet and trailers up to 27 feet. Reservations required in summer and can be made online (recreation.gov) or by calling 877-444-6777 up to five months in advance.

Lower Pines Campground

Located in Yosemite Valley. Open April through October, 60 sites with picnic tables and fire rings, $26 per night, drinking water, flush toilets. None of the sites have RV hookups. Pets permitted. An RV dump station is located at the entrance of nearby Upper Pines Campground. Camping is limited to 14 consecutive days. The campground can accommodate motor homes up to 40 feet and trailers up to 35 feet. Reservations are required and available online (recreation.gov) or by calling 877-444-6777 up to five months in advance.

North Pines Campground

Located in Yosemite Valley. Open March through October, 81 sites with picnic tables and fire rings, $26 per night, drinking water, flush toilets. None of the sites have RV hookups. Pets permitted. An RV dump station is located at the entrance of nearby Upper Pines Campground. Camping is limited to 14 consecutive days. The campground can accommodate motor homes up to 40 feet and trailers up to 35 feet. Reservations are required and can be made online (recreation.gov) or by calling 877-444-6777 up to five months in advance.

Porcupine Flat Campground

Located on Tioga Road (SR-120) about 30 miles east of the Big Oak Flat Entrance Station. Open July through mid-October, 52 sites with picnic tables and fire rings, $12 per night, vault toilets. None of the sites have hookups. There is no potable water available; stream water must be treated. Pets permitted. Camping is limited to 14 consecutive days. The campground can accommodate motor homes up to 24 feet and trailers up to 20 feet (limited availability in first loop only). Sites are available on a first-come, first-served basis; reservations are not accepted.

Tuolumne Meadows Campground

Located on Tioga Road (SR-120) about seven miles west of the Tioga Pass Entrance. Open mid-June to late September, 304 sites with picnic tables and fire rings, drinking water, flush toilets. None of the sites have RV hookups. Equestrian sites available (reservations required). An RV dump station is just west of the campground. Pets permitted. Camping is limited to 14 consecutive days. The campground can accommodate RVs up to 35 feet. Reservations are accepted for half of all sites available and can be made online (recreation.

gov) or by calling 877-444-6777 up to five months in advance.

Upper Pines Campground

Located in Yosemite Valley. Open all year, 238 sites with picnic tables and fire rings, $26 per night, drinking water, flush toilets, dump station. None of the sites have RV hookups. Pets permitted. Camping is limited to 14 consecutive days. The campground can accommodate motor homes up to 35 feet and trailers up to 24 feet. Reservations are required from mid-March through November and can be made online (recreation.gov) or by calling 877-444-6777 up to five months in advance. From December to mid-February, only the first two loops are typically open (about 50 campsites).

Wawona Campground

Located on Wawona Road (SR-41) about six miles north of the South Entrance. Loop A is open all year; Loops B and C are open April through September, 93 sites with picnic tables and fire rings, $26 per night April through September; $18 per night October to April, drinking water, flush toilets. Equestrian sites available. None of the sites have hookups for RVs. Pets permitted. An RV dump station is available in summer on Forest Drive in Wawona. Camping is limited to 14 consecutive days. The campground can accommodate RVs up to 35 feet. Reservations are required during the peak season and can be made online (recreation. gov) or by calling 877-444-6777 up to five months in advance.

White Wolf Campground

Located one mile north of Tioga Road (SR-120) about 22 miles east of the Big Oak Flat Entrance Station. Open July to early September, 74 sites with picnic tables and fire rings, $18 per night, drinking water, flush toilets. None of the sites have hookups. Pets permitted. Camping is limited to 14 consecutive days. The campground can accommodate motor homes up to 27 feet and trailers up to 24 feet. Sites are available on a first-come, first-served basis; reservations are not accepted.

Colorado

KANSAS

NEBRASKA

OKLAHOMA

NEW MEXICO

WYOMING

UTAH

AZ

COLORADO

Burlington

Sterling

34

70

Lamar

287

76

287

Limon

70

50

70

24

Colorado Springs

Fort Collins

34

25

Pueblo

25

Trinidad

Denver

25

Great Sand
Dunes NP&Pr

160

50

Rocky Mountain NP

70

285

285

Alamosa

285

24

160

40

Craig

13

70

Curecanti NRA

50

13

550

Durango

Grand Junction

Black Canyon of the Gunnison NP

Montrose

160

Dinosaur NM

40

50

Colorado NM

Hovenweep NM (see Utah) ■

Mesa Verde NP

D

C

B

A

5

4

3

2

1

Colorado Parks

	Map	Auto Touring	Biking	Boating	Climbing	Fishing	Hiking	Horseback Riding	Hunting	Snow Skiing	Swimming	Visitor Center	Wildlife Viewing
Black Canyon of the Gunnison National Park	B2	•			•	•	•		•			•	•
Colorado National Monument	C1	•	•		•		•		•			•	•
Curecanti National Recreation Area	B2	•		•	•	•	•	•	•	•		•	•
Dinosaur National Monument	D1	•	•		•	•	•					•	•
Great Sand Dunes National Park & Preserve	A3	•					•	•				•	•
Hovenweep National Monument - *see Utah*	A1						•						•
Mesa Verde National Park	A1						•					•	•
Rocky Mountain National Park	D3	•	•		•	•	•		•		•	•	•

PARK DETAILS

Black Canyon of the Gunnison National Park

102 Elk Creek
Gunnison, CO 81230
Phone: 970-641-2337 x205

Description

Black Canyon of the Gunnison National Park features narrow canyon walls that drop nearly vertically over 2,000 feet to the Gunnison River. Numerous scenic overlooks are easily accessed by vehicle or a short walk. There is no bridge across the canyon connecting the North Rim with the South Rim. Visitors should allow two to three hours to drive from one side to the other. The park is one of few designated an International Dark-Sky Park. More than 300,000 people visit this park every year.

Information

The South Rim Visitor Center, which features exhibits on the canyon, is located at Gunnison Point about one mile from the park's entrance. The visitor center is open daily year-round except Thanksgiving and Christmas Day. Hours vary by season but in summer, the hours are 8am to 6pm.

Fees & Season

An entrance fee of $20 is charged per vehicle and is valid for seven days. The South Rim portion of the park is open all year, however, South Rim Road beyond Gunnison Point is closed in winter. The North Rim Road and ranger station are closed in winter. The road typically closes in late November and re-opens in mid-April.

Directions

The park is located in western Colorado about 75 miles southeast of Junction City. The South Rim is seven miles north on SR-347 from the intersection with US-50, east of Montrose. The North Rim is 11 miles southwest of Crawford and is reached by following Black Canyon Road from its intersection with SR-92, south of town. The last seven miles of Black Canyon Road are unpaved.

RV CAMPING

North Rim Campground

Located about 16 miles southwest of Crawford. Open April to mid-November, 13 sites with picnic tables and fire grates, $16 per night, drinking water, vault toilets. There are no hookups provided. The campground can accommodate RVs up to 35 feet. Camping is limited to 14 consecutive days. All sites are available on a first-come, first-served basis; reservations are not accepted. The campground often fills during spring and fall, and occasionally fills during summer months. Water is brought in by truck; filling of RV water tanks is prohibited.

South Rim Campground

Located near the Entrance Station on South Rim Road. Open all year, 88 sites with picnic tables and fire grates, $16 per night for sites without hookups, $22 per night for sites with electric hookups, drinking water, vault toilets. Electric hookups (30-amp) are available in Loop B only. The campground can accommodate RVs up to 35 feet. Camping is limited to 14 consecutive days. Reservations are accepted for sites in Loops A and B and can be made online (recreation.gov) or by calling 877-444-6777. Water is brought in by truck; filling of RV water tanks is prohibited.

PARK DETAILS

Colorado National Monument

1750 Rim Rock Dr
Fruita, CO 81521
Phone: 970-858-3617 x360

Description

Colorado National Monument was established in 1911 and contains about 20,500 acres. Among its features are sheer-walled canyons, soaring arches, unusual formations, dinosaur fossils, and remains of prehistoric Indian cultures. The park receives more than 400,000 visitors every year.

Scenic Drives

Rim Rock Drive travels through the park and can be a bit challenging as it is narrow and steep in some sections with sheer drop-offs. On the east side of the park, motorists may encounter large trucks that use four miles of the roadway to access the nearby community of Glade Park. Bicyclists also use the roadway; use caution especially on tight corners and hills.

Information

Information is available from the Saddlehorn Visitor Center located four miles from the park's entrance. The visitor center is open every day between 9am and 4:30pm except on Christmas Day. Hours are extended in summer from 8am to 6pm. In addition to maps and brochures, the visitor center features educational exhibits, two twelve-minute movies, and a bookstore. The movies are shown on request.

Fees & Season

An entrance fee of $20 per vehicle is charged and is valid for seven days. The park is open year-round.

Directions

Colorado National Monument is in western Colorado, south of Fruita. From I-70 Exit 19, follow SR-340 south about 2.5 miles to the park's entrance.

RV CAMPING

Saddlehorn Campground

Located near the Saddlehorn Visitor Center, four miles from the park's west entrance. Open year-round, 80 sites with picnic tables and charcoal grills, $20 per night, some pull-thru sites, restrooms with flush toilets, drinking water in summer. Pets permitted. The campground can accommodate RVs up to 40 feet. There is a 14-day consecutive stay limit. Campsites in Loop B are reservable from March to October and may be reserved online (recreation.gov) or by calling 877-444-6777 up to six months in advance. Wood fires are not permitted anywhere within the park.

PARK DETAILS

Curecanti National Recreation Area

102 Elk Creek
Gunnison, CO 81230
Phone: 970-641-2337 x205

Description

Curecanti National Recreation Area is a series of three reservoirs along the Gunnison River. The park encompasses nearly 42,000 acres and offers boating, fishing, hiking, camping, and other outdoor activities. The reservoirs are best known for salmon and trout fishing. More than 900,000 visitors come to the park annually.

Information

Information is available from the Elk Creek Visitor Center, which is located 16 miles west of Gunnison on US-50. In summer, the visitor center is open daily from 8am to 6pm. In the spring and fall, it is open daily (except federal holidays) from 8am to 4pm. In winter, the visitor center is open weekdays from 8am to 4pm; it closes on weekends and federal holidays.

Fees & Season

There is no entrance fee to Curecanti National Recreation Area. Visitors traveling to East Portal via the Black Canyon of the Gunnison National Park must pay that park's entrance fee. The recreation area is open all year, weather permitting. East Portal Road typically closes in mid-November and re-opens mid-April.

Directions

The recreation area is in western Colorado. US-50 runs the length of the park between Montrose and Gunnison. Portions of the recreation area are also accessed from SR-149 and SR-92.

RV CAMPING

Cimarron Campground

Located 20 miles east of Montrose on US-50 at the site of a historic narrow gauge railroad town. Open May to mid-October, 21 sites with picnic tables and fire grates, $16 per night, water, flush and vault toilets, dump station. Some amenities are available in summer only. There is a 14-day stay limit. The campground can accommodate RVs up to 35 feet. All sites are first-come, first-served. The campground rarely fills.

Dry Gulch Campground

Located 17 miles west of Gunnison just north of US-50. Open May to mid-October, 9 sites with picnic tables and fire grates, $16 per night, water, vault toilets, horse corral. There is a 14-day stay limit. The campground can accommodate RVs up to 35 feet. All sites are first-come, first-served; reservations are not accepted.

Elk Creek Campground

Located 16 miles west of Gunnison on US-50. Open all year, 160 sites with picnic tables and fire grates, $16 per night, electric hookups available in Loop D for $22 per night, water, flush and vault toilets, showers, dump station, marina, restaurant, boat ramp, fish cleaning station. Some amenities available only during summer. There is a 14-day stay limit. The campground can accommodate large RVs over 35 feet. Reservations accepted (and recommended in summer) for sites in Loops A and D. Reservations may be made online at recreation.gov or by calling 877-444-6777.

Lake Fork Campground

Located on SR-92 about 27 miles west of Gunnison. Open April to mid-October, 90 sites with picnic tables and fire grates, $16 per night, water, flush and vault toilets, dump station, marina, boat ramp, fish cleaning station. Some amenities available in summer only. There is a 14-day stay limit. The campground can accommodate large RVs over 35 feet. Reservations are accepted and may be made online at recreation.gov or by calling 877-444-6777.

Ponderosa Campground

Located at the northwest end of the Soap Creek Arm of Blue Mesa Reservoir off US-50 and SR-92. Access road is gravel and can become hazardous or impassable when wet. Open May to mid-October, 28 sites with picnic tables and fire grates, $16 per night, water, vault toilets, boat ramp, horse corral. There is a 14-day stay limit. The campground can accommodate RVs up to 35 feet. All sites are available on a first-come, first-served basis only; reservations are not accepted.

Red Creek Campground

Located 19 miles west of Gunnison of US-50. Open May to mid-October, one site with picnic table and fire grate, $16 per night, water, vault toilets. There is a 14-day stay limit. RVs longer than 22 feet are not recommended due to a lack of space to turn around. Reservations are not accepted.

Stevens Creek Campground

Located 12 miles west of Gunnison on US-50. Open late May to mid-October, 53 sites with picnic tables and fire grates, $16 per night, water, vault toilets, boat ramp, fish cleaning station. There is a 14-day stay limit. The campground can accommodate large RVs over 35 feet. Reservations are accepted and may be made online at recreation.gov or by calling 877-444-6777.

PARK DETAILS

Dinosaur National Monument

4545 Highway 40
Dinosaur, CO 81610
Phone: 435-781-7700

Description

Established in 1915, Dinosaur National Monument encompasses over 210,000 acres of land across Colorado and Utah. The park features deep, narrow gorges, sandstone cliffs along the Green and Yampa Rivers, and one of the world's largest concentrations of fossilized dinosaur bones. Dinosaur fossils are located in the Utah portion of the park in Quarry Exhibit Hall. More than 250,000 people come to the park each year.

Information

Information is available from the Canyon Area Visitor Center (park headquarters) located two miles east of Dinosaur, Colorado, on US-40. Exhibits and a ten-minute orientation program provide information about the monument's scenic canyon country. The visitor center is open daily, 9am to 5pm, from late May to early October. Information is also available from the Quarry Visitor Center, which is located seven miles north of Jensen, Utah, off SR-149. Near this visitor center is the Quarry Exhibit Hall and the famous wall of dinosaur bones. The visitor center remains open year-round (except holidays in winter).

Fees & Season

An entrance fee of $25 per vehicle is collected and is valid for seven days. The monument is typically open year-round but some roads and facilities are closed during the winter months.

Directions

The park is located in northeast Utah and northwest Colorado. There are two primary points of entry into the park. In Jensen, Utah, SR-149 provides access to the western portion of the park. Harpers Corner Road, near Dinosaur, Colorado, provides access to the central portion of the park.

RV CAMPING

Gates of Lodore Campground

Located in the extreme northernmost part of the park about 10 miles west of SR-318 via CR-34. Open year-round, 19 sites with picnic tables and campfire rings with grill, $10 per night, water (mid-May to early October), vault toilets. Water is available mid-May to early October; fees reduced when water is turned off. Access road may become impassable in winter. All sites available on a first-come, first-served basis. The campground rarely fills.

Green River Campground

Located along SR-149 about ten miles northeast of Jensen, Utah. Open early April to late October (weather permitting), 79 sites with picnic tables and campfire rings with grill, $18 per night, water, restrooms with flush toilets. Reservations are accepted for some sites and can be made online at recreation.gov or by calling 877-444-6777.

PARK DETAILS

Great Sand Dunes National Park & Preserve

11999 State Highway 150
Mosca, CO 81146
Phone: 719-378-6395

Description

The 149,500-acre park features the tallest sand dunes in North America surrounded by grasslands, wetlands, and mountains. The park also features several hiking trails and a four-wheel drive route to Medano Pass. Many park visitors enjoy sandboarding or sledding down the dunes; equipment is available for rent nearby. Over 270,000 people come to experience this park each year.

Information

Information may be obtained from the park's visitor center, which features a 20-minute video, interactive exhibits, restrooms, vending machines, and park store.

The visitor center is open daily year-round except federal holidays in winter. Summer hours are 8:30am to 5pm daily. The rest of the year, hours are 9am to 4:30pm.

Fees & Season

An entrance fee of $25 is charged that is valid for one week. The park remains open all year.

Directions

The park is about 30 miles northeast of Alamosa via US-160 and SR-150.

RV CAMPING

Piñon Flats Campground

Located one mile north of the visitor center. Open April through October, 88 sites with picnic tables and fire grates, $20 per night, water, restrooms with flush toilets. A dump station and water hoses are available in warmer months. A camp store sells firewood and other items. Pets are permitted. The campground can accommodate RVs up to 35 feet. There is a 14-day stay limit. Reservations are required during peak season (May to late September) and may be made online at recreation.gov or by calling 877-444-6777.

PARK DETAILS

Mesa Verde National Park

PO Box 8
Mesa Verde, CO 81330
Phone: 970-529-4465

Description

Mesa Verde National Park protects and preserves nearly 5,000 known archeological sites, including 600 cliff dwellings. Ancestral Pueblo people inhabited this region for over 700 years from AD 550 to 1300. Guided tours are offered at several cliff dwellings. Self-guided tours are also available. The park receives more than 500,000 visitors each year.

Information

Information can be obtained from the Mesa Verde Visitor and Research Center located at the park's entrance. The visitor center is typically open all year except on Thanksgiving, Christmas, and New Year's Day. Hours vary by season; in summer the hours are 7:30am to 7pm. Tickets for guided tours can be purchased here.

Fees & Season

The park remains open all year long. An entrance fee of $25 is charged May through October; the fee is $15 the remainder of the year. The entrance fee is valid for seven days.

Directions

Mesa Verde National Park is in southwest Colorado about 36 miles west of Durango and 10 miles east of Cortez via US-160.

RV CAMPING

Morefield Campground

The campground is located four miles from the park entrance. Open mid-April to mid-October, 267 sites with picnic tables and grill, 15 full-hookup sites, $30 and up, restrooms, showers, laundry, dump station, gas station, gift shop, groceries, cafe. The campground can accommodate RVs up to 46 feet long. There is a 14-day stay limit. Reservations are accepted (required for full-hookup sites) and can be made by calling 800-449-2288 or online at visitmesaverde.com. The campground rarely fills.

PARK DETAILS

Rocky Mountain National Park

1000 US Highway 36
Estes Park, CO 80517
Phone: 970-586-1206

Description

Rocky Mountain National Park encompasses over 265,000 acres of some of the most beautiful mountain scenery in Colorado. Trail Ridge Road crosses the park and the Continental Divide; spectacular views of the surrounding mountain peaks are offered along the route. The park also features over 300 miles of hiking trails, valleys of wildflowers, and abundant wildlife. This popular park receives over four million visitors every year.

Scenic Drives

Trail Ridge Road/Beaver Meadow Road is an All-American Road and is the highest continuously paved road in America. Overlooks along the route offer spectacular views of peaks ranging from 12,000 to over 14,000 feet. Eleven miles of the route roam above tree line in the alpine tundra. For current road conditions, call the park's Trail Ridge Road recorded status line at 970-586-1222. The message is updated with any changes in the road's status and is available 24 hours a day.

Information

Information is available at four visitor centers within the park. Alpine Visitor Center is located at Fall River Pass at the junction of Trail Ridge and Old Fall River roads. It is open daily from 9am to 5pm during summer. Beaver Meadows Visitor Center is open daily all year except Thanksgiving and Christmas days; hours vary by season. The visitor center is on US-36, three miles west of Estes Park. Fall River Visitor Center is five miles west of Estes Park along US-34 and is typically open daily late spring to mid-fall. Kawuneeche Visitor Center is just north of Grand Lake on US-34; it is typically open daily all year except Thanksgiving and Christmas days.

Fees & Season

The park remains open year-round; summer and fall are the busiest seasons in the park. A one-day pass is available for $25; a seven-day pass costs $35 and is valid for seven consecutive days (including date of purchase).

Directions

Rocky Mountain National Park is in north-central Colorado about 70 miles northwest of Denver. From I-25 Exit 257 in Loveland, go west approximately 33 miles on US-34 then follow US-36 west for four miles to the Beaver Meadows Entrance.

RV CAMPING

Aspenglen Campground

Situated in a pine forest near Fall River just inside the Fall River Entrance on US-34. Open late May to late September, 36 sites with picnic tables and fire grates, $26 per night, drinking water, restrooms with flush toilets. The campground can accommodate RVs up to 30 feet. There is a seven-day stay limit. Pets are permitted in the campground. Ranger-led evening programs offered in summer. Reservations highly recommended and may be made online at recreation.gov or by calling 877-444-6777. The campground is usually filled every night.

Glacier Basin Campground

Located seven miles west of Beaver Meadows Visitor Center on Bear Lake Road. Open late May to early September, 61 sites with picnic tables and fire grates, $26 per night, drinking water, restrooms with flush toilets, dump station. The campground can accommodate RVs up to 35 feet. There is a seven-day stay limit. Pets are permitted in the campground. Ranger-led evening programs offered in summer. Reservations are recommended and may be made online at recreation.gov or by calling 877-444-6777.

Moraine Park Campground

Located on Bear Lake Road about seven miles west of Estes Park. Open all year, 97 sites with picnic tables and fire grates, $26 per night during the peak season ($18 per night off season), drinking water, flush and vault toilets, dump station. The campground can accommodate RVs up to 40 feet. There is a seven-day stay limit in summer (14 days otherwise). Pets permitted. Ranger-led evening programs offered in summer. Reservations recommended and may be made online at recreation.gov or by calling 877-444-6777.

Timber Creek Campground

Located 10 miles north of Grand Lake on US-34. Open late May to early November, 98 sites with picnic tables and fire grates, $26 per night, drinking water, restrooms with flush toilets, dump station. The campground can accommodate RVs up to 30 feet. There is a seven-day stay limit in summer. Pets are permitted in the campground. Ranger-led evening programs offered in summer. Campsites are available on a first-come, first-served basis; reservations are not accepted.

Florida

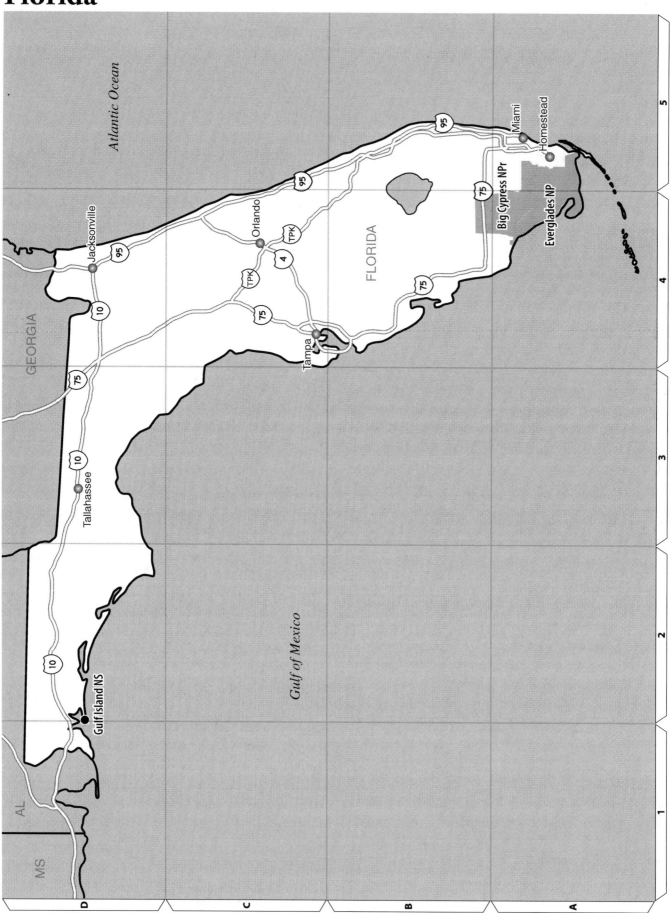

Florida Parks

	Map	Auto Touring	Biking	Boating	Climbing	Fishing	Hiking	Horseback Riding	Hunting	Snow Skiing	Swimming	Visitor Center	Wildlife Viewing
Big Cypress National Preserve	A4	•	•			•	•		•			•	•
Everglades National Park	A5		•	•		•	•					•	•
Gulf Islands National Seashore	D2		•	•		•	•	•			•	•	•

PARK DETAILS

Big Cypress National Preserve

33100 Tamiami Trail E
Ochopee, FL 34141
Phone: 239-695-2000

Description

Over 729,000 acres of the Big Cypress Swamp are preserved in this park. The park is home to a variety of wildlife, including the Florida panther. It is also home to nine federally listed endangered species including the West Indian Manatee, the eastern indigo snake, and the Florida Sandhill Crane. The park is one of few designated an International Dark-Sky Park. Approximately one million people visit the park each year.

Information

Information is available from the Big Cypress Swamp Welcome Center, which is on US-41 about 35 miles east of Naples. Information is also available from the Oasis Visitor Center, also on US-41 about 53 miles east of Naples. Features include a 15-minute movie about the preserve, a wildlife exhibit, and book sales. Both are open year-round but close on Christmas Day.

Fees & Season

The park is open all year but, from time to time, the superintendent implements area closures to protect resources or to ensure visitor safety. There is no entrance fee to access the preserve but fees are collected from some facilities and the processing of off-road vehicle permits.

Directions

Big Cypress National Preserve is in southern Florida between Miami and Naples and is accessible from US-41.

RV CAMPING

Bear Island Campground

Located 20 miles north of US-41 via Turner River Rd (CR-839). Open all year, 40 sites with picnic tables and fire rings, $10 per night, vault toilets, no water. Pets permitted. Twelve sites are open year-round, the rest are open from mid-August to mid-April. There is a 14-day stay limit. Sites are available on a first-come, first-served basis; reservations are not accepted.

Burns Lake Campground

Located one mile north of US-41 about six miles east of the Big Cypress Swamp Welcome Center. Open mid-August to late January, eight sites with picnic tables and fire rings, $24 per night, vault toilets, no water. Pets permitted. The campground can accommodate RVs up to 50 feet. There is a 10-day stay limit from January through April; 14 days May through December. Reservations are accepted and can be made online at recreation.gov or by calling 877-444-6777.

Midway Campground

Located along US-41 about three miles east of the Oasis Visitor Center. Open year-round, 26 sites with 30-amp electric hookups, $30 per night, picnic tables, drinking water, restrooms, dump station. Pets permitted. The campground can accommodate RVs up to 45 feet. There is a 10-day stay limit from January through April; 14 days the rest of the year. Reservations are accepted and can be made online at recreation.gov or by calling 877-444-6777.

Mitchell Landing Campground

Located west of Fortymile Bend along CR-94. Open mid-August to mid-April, 11 sites with picnic tables and fire rings, $24 per night, vault toilets, no water. Pets permitted. The campground can accommodate RVs up to 30 feet. There is a 10-day stay limit from January to mid-April; 14 days the rest of the season. Sites are available on a first-come, first-served basis; reservations are not accepted.

Monument Lake Campground

Located along US-41 about 48 miles east of Naples. Open mid-August to mid-April, 26 sites with picnic tables, $28 per night, restrooms, drinking water. Pets permitted. There is a 10-day stay limit from January to mid-April; 14 days the rest of the season. Reservations are accepted and can be made online at recreation.gov or by calling 877-444-6777.

PARK DETAILS

Everglades National Park

40001 State Road 9336
Homestead, FL 33034
Phone: 305-242-7700

Description

Everglades National Park protects 1.5 million acres of subtropical wilderness. The park provides important habitat for numerous rare and endangered species like the manatee, American crocodile, and the Florida panther. Ranger-led walks and talks are offered year-round; boat tours are also available. The park receives about one million visitors every year.

Information

Information is available from four visitor centers. Ernest Coe Visitor Center is on SR-9336 near Homestead, Florida. It is open year-round and offers educational displays, orientation films, and brochures. The Flamingo Visitor Center is about 38 miles south of the park's main entrance near Homestead, Florida, along SR-9336. It is open daily mid-November to mid-April; intermittently the rest of the year. There are educational displays, brochures, and backcountry permits available at this location. The Gulf Coast Visitor Center is located five miles south of US-41 on SR-29 in Everglades City. It remains open year-round and offers educational displays, a park video, brochures, and backcountry permits. Shark Valley Visitor Center is located along US-41 about 25 miles west of the Florida Turnpike in Miami. It remains open year-round and offers educational displays, a park video, and brochures.

Fees & Season

The park remains open year-round. During the busy, dry season in winter, most facilities are open and a full range of tours and programs are offered. During the slow, wet season in summer, facilities may have limited hours or close altogether, and recreational opportunities may be at a minimum. An entrance fee of $30 is charged and is valid for seven days.

Directions

The park's main entrance is off US-1 in Homestead, Florida, which is about 30 miles southwest of Miami.

RV CAMPING

Flamingo Campground

Located near the Flamingo Visitor Center on the shores of Florida Bay. Open year-round, 234 sites with picnic tables and grills ($20 per night), 41 sites have electric hookups ($30 per night), restrooms with flush toilets, drinking water, showers, dump station, amphitheater, picnic area. The campground can accommodate RVs up to 45 feet. Reservations are required for electric sites during the peak season (December to April) and can be made online at flamingoeverglades.com or by calling 855-708-2207.

Long Pine Key Campground

Located seven miles from the park's main entrance near Homestead. Open October through April, 108 sites with picnic tables and grills, $20 per night, restrooms, showers, potable water, dump station. The campground can accommodate RVs up to 36 feet. Sites are only available on a first-come, first-served basis; reservations not accepted.

PARK DETAILS

Gulf Islands National Seashore

1801 Gulf Breeze Parkway
Gulf Breeze, FL 32563
Phone: 850-934-2600

Description

Gulf Islands National Seashore consists of 13 separate units stretching 160 miles from Cat Island, Mississippi, to the eastern tip of Santa Rosa Island in Florida. The 135,607-acre park was established in 1971. The park features white sandy beaches, historic forts, and nature trails. Approximately four million people come to the park every year.

Information

Information is available from three visitor center locations, all of which close on Thanksgiving, Christmas, and New Year's Day. Fort Barrancas Visitor Center is located on Pensacola Naval Air Station and is typically open Thursday through Monday from 9am to 4:15pm. William M. Colmer Visitor Center is located in the Davis Bayou area near Ocean Springs, Mississippi; it is open daily from 9am to 4:30pm. The park's headquarters is located in the Naval Live Oaks Area on US-98 in Gulf Breeze, Florida. The headquarters is open weekdays from 8:30am to 4:30pm.

Fees & Season

An entrance fee of $25 per vehicle is charged that is valid for seven days. All areas of the park are open year-round but operating hours vary seasonally from unit to unit.

Directions

Gulf Islands National Seashore is divided into the Florida District, located in the northwest panhandle, and the Mississippi District, located in coastal Mississippi. You can drive to some park areas but must take a boat to others. In Florida, all of the areas are accessible by car, located on Santa Rosa Island. In Mississippi, only the Davis Bayou Area located in Ocean Springs is accessible by car. Visitors may use the passenger ferry to reach West Ship Island, use their own vessels, or hire a National Park Service licensed boat operator for transportation to the islands.

RV CAMPING

Davis Bayou Campground

Located near Ocean Springs, Mississippi, two miles south of US-90. Open year-round, 51 sites with water and 50-amp electric hookups, picnic tables and fire rings, $22 per night, restrooms with flush toilets, showers, dump station. Pets permitted. Campers may stay no more than 30 days annually and no more than 14 days during the campground's peak period of January 1 through March 31. The campground can accommodate RVs up to 45 feet at some sites. Reservations are accepted and can be made online at recreation.gov or by calling 877-444-6777.

Fort Pickens Campground

Located on the west end of Santa Rosa Island. Open year-round, 200 sites with water and 50-amp electric hookups, picnic tables and fire rings, $40 per night, restrooms with flush toilets, dump station. Pets permitted. Campers may stay no more than 42 days annually and no more than 14 days during the campground's peak period of March 1 through Labor Day. The campground can accommodate RVs up to 50 feet. Reservations are accepted and can be made online at recreation.gov or by calling 877-444-6777.

Idaho

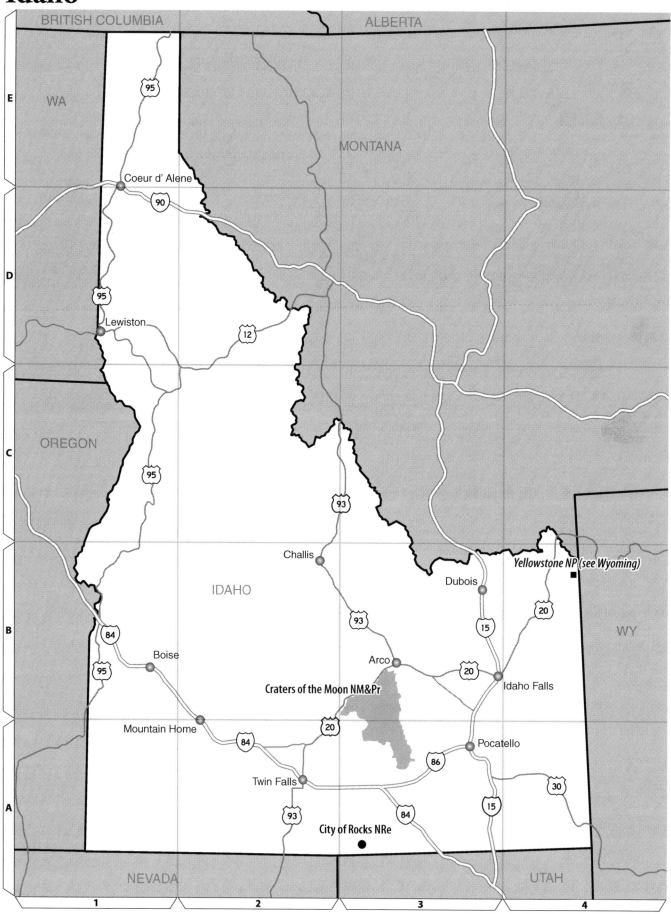

Idaho Parks

	Map	Auto Touring	Biking	Boating	Climbing	Fishing	Hiking	Horseback Riding	Hunting	Snow Skiing	Swimming	Visitor Center	Wildlife Viewing
City of Rocks National Reserve	A3	•	•		•		•	•	•			•	•
Craters of the Moon National Monument & Preserve	B3	•	•				•		•			•	•
Yellowstone National Park - *see Wyoming*	B4	•	•	•		•	•	•		•		•	•

PARK DETAILS

City of Rocks National Reserve

PO Box 169
Almo, ID 83312
Phone: 208-824-5901

Description

Established in 1988, the 14,407-acre park features scenic granite spires and sculptured rock formations. Remnants of the California Trail are still visible in the area. Emigrants of the California Trail described the rocks here as "a city of tall spires," "steeple rocks," and "the silent city." Approximately 90,000 people come to experience this park every year.

Information

Information is available from the visitor center in Almo. Brochures, climbing guides, historic trail information, camping information, books, and gifts are available. The visitor center is open daily from mid-April to late October; hours are 8am to 4:30pm. During the off-season, the visitor center is open Tuesday through Saturday; hours are 8am to 4:30pm. It closes on federal winter holidays, too.

Fees & Season

No entrance fee is charged. The park remains open year-round but some roads may be impassable from November through April; all roads within the park are gravel.

Directions

City of Rocks National Reserve is in southern Idaho about 70 miles southeast of Twin Falls. From I-84 Exit 216, go south on SR-77 for 23 miles and then continue southward for 16 miles on Elba-Almo Rd.

RV CAMPING

City of Rocks National Reserve offers a total of 64 campsites among the granite formations throughout the park. Of these, only six can accommodate RVs. One site can accommodate RVs up to 40 feet (typically used by the campground host); three can accommodate RVs up to 25 feet. The remaining two sites can accommodate smaller RVs of 18 and 20 feet. The camping fee is $12.72 and the reservation fee is $10.60. Each site has a picnic table and fire grill. Potable water is available from the hand pump well located along Emery Canyon Road about one mile north of Bath Rock. Water is also available from the hand pump well at Bath Rock and at the visitor center. All other water should be treated before using. Clean vault toilets are centrally located. Pets are welcome but must be on a leash. There is a stay limit of 14 days. Reservations are accepted and can be made online at reserveamerica.com or by calling 888-922-6743. RV camping is also available in nearby Castle Rocks State Park.

PARK DETAILS

Craters of the Moon National Monument & Preserve

PO Box 29
Arco, ID 83213
Phone: 208-527-1300

Description

Established in 1924, the 750,000-acre park preserves more than 25 volcanic cones and 60 different lava flows. The lava landscape is the result of periodic eruptions along the Great Rift, a chain of cracks and fissures nearly 52 miles long. Numerous hiking trails, from easy to strenuous, offer opportunities to further explore the harsh landscape. The park is one of few designated an International Dark-Sky Park.

Information

Information is available from the Robert Limbert Visitor Center, located near the park's entrance. The visitor center is open year-round. Hours are 8am to 6pm daily in summer and 8am to 4:30pm daily in the off-season. It closes on federal holidays in winter. Features include exhibits, films, bookstore, vending machines, and restrooms.

Fees & Season

The park is open every day but some park facilities and the loop road are closed during the winter. When the loop road is open, an entrance fee of $20 per vehicle is charged.

Directions

Craters of the Moon National Monument and Preserve is in central Idaho about 90 miles northeast of Twin Falls. The park's entrance is along US-20/US-26/US-93 about 19 miles south of Arco.

RV CAMPING

Lava Flow Campground

Located near the park's entrance and visitor center. Open mid-April through November weather permitting, 42 sites with picnic tables and fire grills, $15 per night ($8 per night when water is shut off), water, restrooms. Pets welcome. There is a 14-day stay limit. Large RVs can be accommodated in a limited number of sites. All sites are available on a first-come, first served basis; reservations are not accepted. Wood fires are prohibited.

Indiana

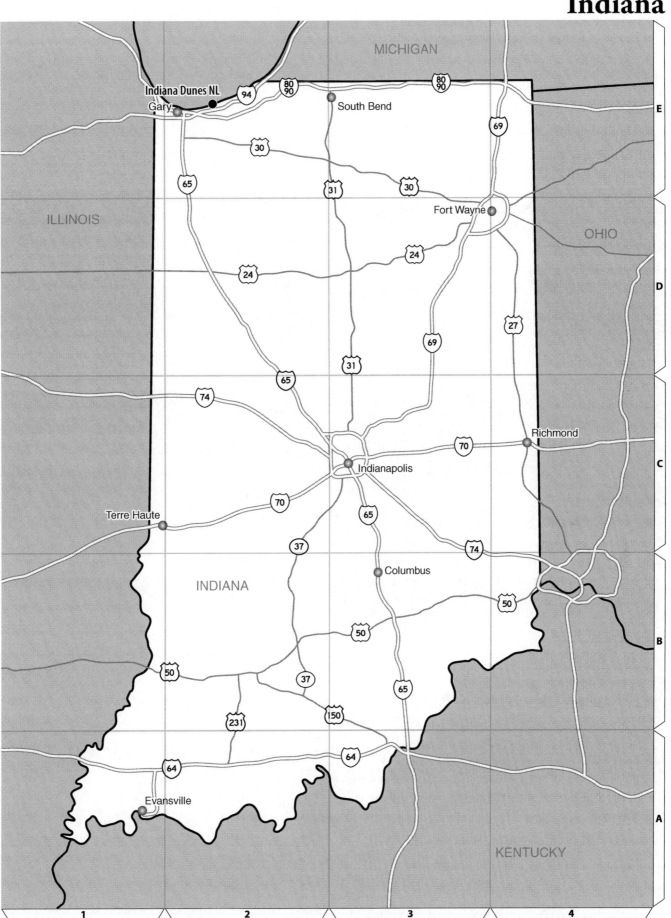

Indiana Parks

Indiana Parks	Map	Auto Touring	Biking	Boating	Climbing	Fishing	Hiking	Horseback Riding	Hunting	Snow Skiing	Swimming	Visitor Center	Wildlife Viewing
Indiana Dunes National Lakeshore	E2	•	•			•	•	•			•	•	•

PARK DETAILS

Indiana Dunes National Lakeshore

1100 N Mineral Springs Rd
Porter, IN 46304
Phone: 219-395-1882

Description

Indiana Dunes National Lakeshore features miles of beaches, sand dunes, woodland forests, an 1830's French Canadian homestead, and a working 1900-era farm combine. The park also offers nearly 50 miles of hiking trails. Established in 1966, the park protects and preserves over 15,000 acres. More than two million people visit the park every year.

Information

Information is available from the visitor center in Porter on SR-49 about one mile north of I-94 Exit 26B. The visitor center is open daily except winter holidays. Summer hours are 8am to 6pm; winter hours are 8:30am to 4:30pm. Features include a short orientation video, bookstore, and brochures describing the area's attractions.

Fees & Season

The park remains open year-round. No entrance fee is charged.

Directions

The park is located in northwest Indiana, east of Gary. The park can be accessed from several points along US-12.

RV CAMPING

Dunewood Campground

Located along US-12 about 6 miles northeast of SR-49 and the visitor center. Open April to through October, 54 sites with picnic tables and fire grates, $25 per night, restrooms, hot showers. Pets permitted. An automated on-site registration and payment kiosk only accepts MasterCard, Visa, or Discover; cash or checks are not accepted. There is a 14-day length of stay limit. All sites are available on a first-come, first-served basis; reservations are not accepted. During most summer weekends, the campground is full by Friday afternoon.

Kentucky

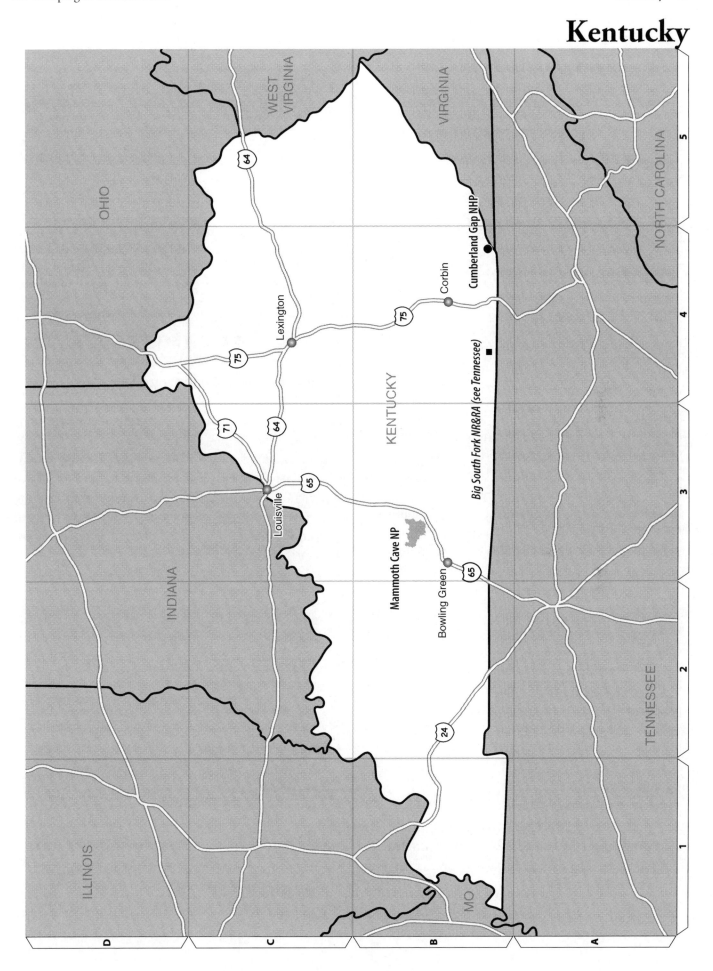

Kentucky Parks

	Map	Auto Touring	Biking	Boating	Climbing	Fishing	Hiking	Horseback Riding	Hunting	Snow Skiing	Swimming	Visitor Center	Wildlife Viewing
Big South Fork National River and RA - *see Tennessee*	B4		•	•	•	•	•	•	•		•	•	•
Cumberland Gap National Historical Park	B4	•	•					•	•			•	•
Mammoth Cave National Park	B3	•	•	•		•	•	•				•	•

PARK DETAILS

Cumberland Gap National Historical Park

91 Bartlett Park Rd
Middlesboro, KY 40965
Phone: 606-248-2817

Description

This mountain pass developed into a main artery for settlers and was an important military objective in the Civil War. The 20,454-acre park was established in 1940 and offers mountain scenery, 85 miles of trails, and wildlife viewing among other activities. Pinnacle Overlook is at an elevation of 2,440 feet and offers a beautiful view into Kentucky, Virginia, and Tennessee. Nearly one million people come to the park each year.

Information

Information is available from the park's visitor center located just south of Middlesboro, Kentucky, along US-25E. The visitor center is open daily 8am to 5pm from mid-March to mid-November. Hours are 9am to 4pm the rest of the year; it closes on Christmas Day. It houses a museum with hands-on exhibits, book sales outlet, and an auditorium featuring two films.

Fees & Season

Cumberland Gap remains open year-round but the road leading to Pinnacle Overlook may close periodically due to inclement weather. There is no entrance fee charged. Fees are charged for Gap Cave Tour and Hensley Settlement Tour.

Directions

Cumberland Gap National Historical Park is in southeast Kentucky, southwest Virginia, and northeastern Tennessee. The park is accessible from points along US-25E and US-58.

RV CAMPING

Wilderness Road Campground

Located in Virginia along US-58 about two miles east of US-25E. Open all year, 160 sites with picnic tables and fire grates, $14 per night, 41 sites have electric hookups (20/30/50-amp) for $20 per night, water, restrooms with flush toilets, hot showers, dump station, amphitheater. There is a 14-day stay limit. The campground can accommodate RVs up to 50 feet. All sites are available on a first-come, first-served basis; reservations are not accepted.

PARK DETAILS

Mammoth Cave National Park

PO Box 7
Mammoth Cave, KY 42259
Phone: 270-758-2180

Description

Mammoth Cave National Park was established in 1941 to preserve the longest recorded cave system in the world; more than 400 miles explored. It also protects and preserves the scenic river valleys of the Green and Nolin Rivers. The park encompasses nearly 53,000 acres and receives more than 500,000 visitors every year.

Information

Information is available from the park's visitor center located along Mammoth Cave Parkway, north of Park City. The visitor center is open all year except on Christmas Day. In summer, hours are typically 8am to 6:30pm; hours vary the rest of the year. Features include exhibits of cave exploration, films, and a bookstore.

Fees & Season

The park is open year-round. There is no entrance fee but fees are charged for cave tours, camping, and selected picnic shelter reservations. Cave tour fees range from $8 to $60; reservations are strongly recommended as cave tours frequently sell out.

Directions

Mammoth Cave National Park is in central Kentucky about 30 miles northeast of Bowling Green. The park is accessible from various points along SR-70.

RV CAMPING

Mammoth Cave Campground

Located near the park's visitor center. Open year-round, 105 sites with picnic tables and grills, $20 per night, potable water, restrooms with flush toilets. Nearby camp store has food, ice, firewood, showers, laundry, and a dump station. Pets welcome. The campground can accommodate motor homes up to 38 feet and trailers up to 26 feet at some sites. There is a 14-day maximum stay limit. Reservations are accepted and may be made online at recreation.gov or by calling 877-444-6777.

Maine

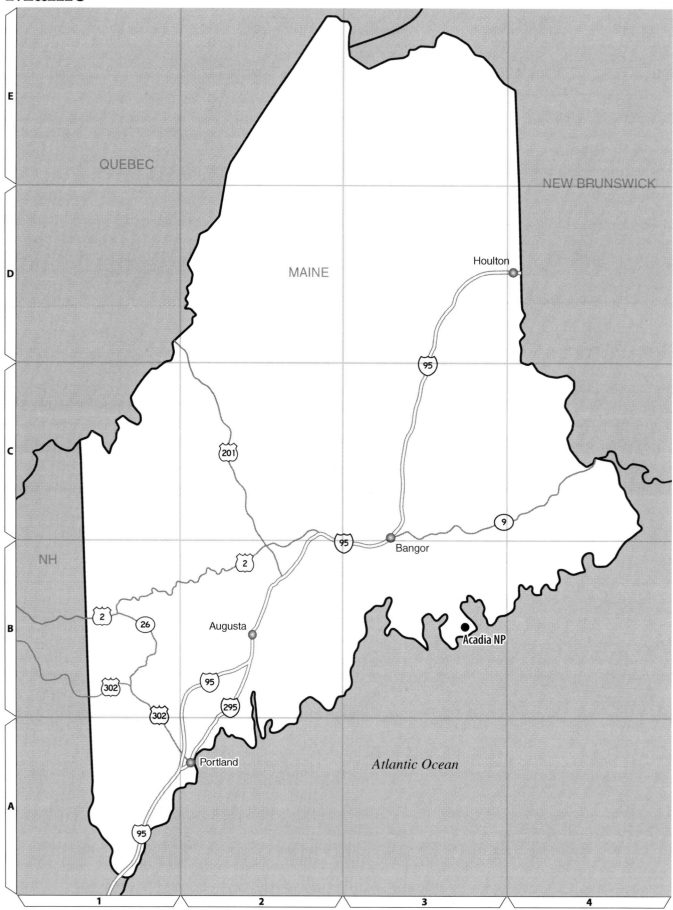

Maine Parks

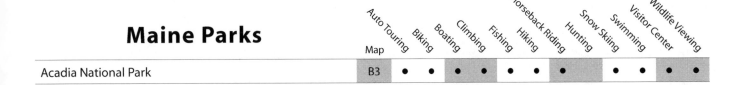

	Map	Auto Touring	Biking	Boating	Climbing	Fishing	Hiking	Horseback Riding	Hunting	Snow Skiing	Swimming	Visitor Center	Wildlife Viewing
Acadia National Park	B3	●	●	●	●	●	●		●		●	●	●	●

PARK DETAILS

Acadia National Park

PO Box 177
Bar Harbor, ME 04609
Phone: 207-288-3338

Description

Acadia National Park was the first national park established east of the Mississippi River. It protects over 47,000 acres of granite-domed mountains, woodlands, lakes and ponds, and ocean shoreline. Those interested in hiking will find more than 150 miles of trails to explore. The park is among the top ten national parks visited, receiving 3.5 million visitors annually.

Information

Information is available from the Hulls Cove Visitor Center, located along SR-3 north of Bar Harbor. The visitor center is open daily from mid-April through October. In April, May, June, September, and October, visitor center hours are 8:30am to 4:30pm. In July and August, visitor center hours are 8am to 6pm. The visitor center features a 15-minute film about the park and a three-dimensional map of the island.

Fees & Season

The park remains open year-round but the primary loop road closes in winter generally from December to mid-April. Other park roads are usually closed from mid-November to mid-May. An entrance fee of $30 per vehicle is charged from May to October. The fee is valid for seven days.

Directions

Acadia National Park is in northern coastal Maine about 16 miles south of Ellsworth via SR-3.

RV CAMPING

Blackwoods Campground

Located on SR-3 about five miles south of Bar Harbor. Open all year, 61 sites with picnic tables and fire rings, $30 per night, water, restrooms with flush toilets, dump station. Pets welcome. From December through March, a limited number of campsites are available for primitive camping only; there is no drive-in access to the campground during this time. There is a 14-day stay limit. The campground can accommodate RVs up to 35 feet. Reservations are recommended and can be made online at recreation.gov or by calling 877-444-6777.

Schoodic Woods Campground

Located on the Schoodic Peninsula about three miles southeast of Winter Harbor near the park entrance. Open late May to mid-October, 34 sites, picnic tables, fire rings, restrooms with showers, dump station, amphitheater. Camping fee is $30 for a small RV site with 20-amp service; $36 for an RV site with electric only (20/30/50 amp); $40 for an RV site with electric and water (20/30/50 amp). Pets welcome. There is a 14-day stay limit. Reservations are recommended and can be made online at recreation.gov or by calling 877-444-6777.

Seawall Campground

Located along SR-102A about four miles south of Southwest Harbor. Open late May through September, 40 sites with picnic tables and fire rings, $30 per night, water, restrooms with flush toilets, dump station. Pets welcome. There is a 14-day stay limit. The campground can accommodate RVs up to 35 feet. Reservations are recommended and can be made online at recreation.gov or by calling 877-444-6777.

Maryland

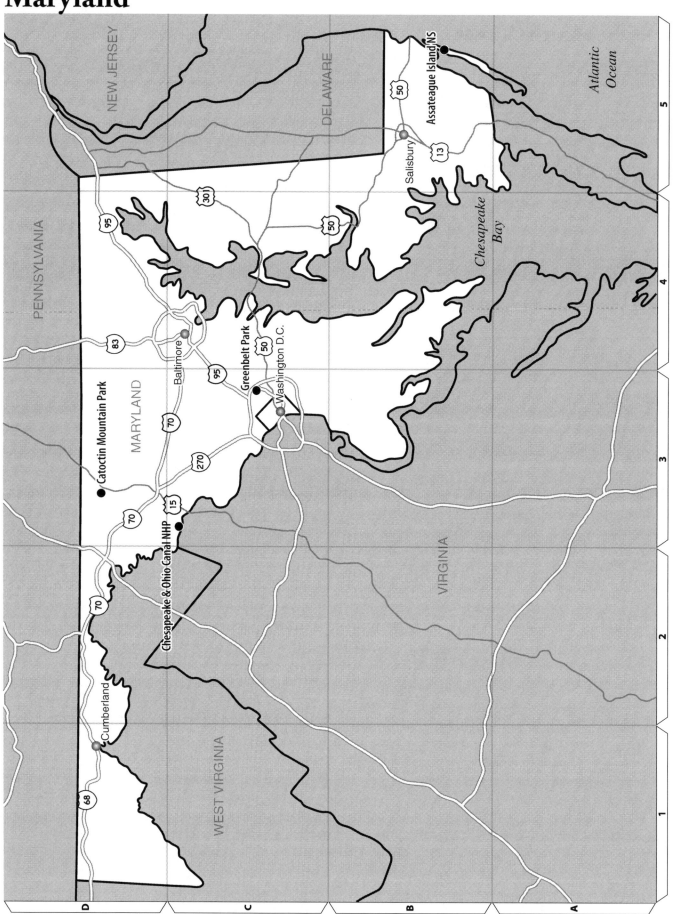

NEW JERSEY

Atlantic Ocean

DELAWARE

Assateague Island NS

50

13

Salisbury

301

95

Chesapeake Bay

50

PENNSYLVANIA

83

Baltimore

95

Greenbelt Park

50

Washington D.C.

MARYLAND

Catoctin Mountain Park

70

270

15

Chesapeake & Ohio Canal NHP

70

VIRGINIA

WEST VIRGINIA

Cumberland

68

70

Maryland Parks

	Map	Auto Touring	Biking	Boating	Climbing	Fishing	Hiking	Horseback Riding	Hunting	Snow Skiing	Swimming	Visitor Center	Wildlife Viewing
Assateague Island National Seashore	B5		•	•		•	•	•	•		•	•	•
Catoctin Mountain Park	D3				•	•	•		•			•	•
Chesapeake & Ohio Canal National Historical Park	C3		•	•	•	•	•		•			•	•
Greenbelt Park	C3		•				•		•			•	•

PARK DETAILS

Assateague Island National Seashore

7206 National Seashore Ln
Berlin, MD 21811
Phone: 410-641-1441

Description

Assateague Island National Seashore was established in 1965 and encompasses 39,723 acres of land and water. Assateague is a 37-mile long barrier island; a portion of the park extends into Virginia and is managed by the Fish and Wildlife Service as Chincoteague National Wildlife Refuge. Two herds of wild horses inhabit the island. The Maryland herd roams freely in part of the park; the Virginia herd roams in large fenced areas in the wildlife refuge. The park also features 12 miles of beach in Maryland, and a small portion in Virginia, open to over-sand vehicles. More than two million people come to this park every year.

Information

Information is available from the Assateague Island Visitor Center located along SR-611, before the Verrazzano Bridge entrance into the park. The visitor center is open daily March to December from 9am to 5pm (it closes on Thanksgiving and Christmas days). In January and February, the center is open Thursday through Monday between 9am and 5pm. Features include beachcombing exhibits, educational brochures, nature films, and a marine aquarium.

A visitor center is also in Chincoteague National Wildlife Refuge at Toms Cove. This visitor center is open daily from March to November and Friday through Monday in winter. Summer hours are 9am to 5pm and 9am to 4pm the rest of the year. Features include beachcombing exhibits, educational brochures, a marine aquarium and touch tank.

Fees & Season

The park remains open year-round. An entrance fee of $20 is charged and is valid for seven days. Entrance passes may be used in both Assateague Island National Seashore and Chincoteague National Wildlife Refuge.

Directions

Assateague Island National Seashore is in southeast Maryland, eight miles south of Ocean City. From Berlin, Maryland, follow SR-376 about four miles and then SR-611 into the park. The southern portion in Virginia is accessible via SR-175 off US-13.

RV CAMPING

Assateague Island National Seashore Campground

Camping is available only in the Maryland portion of the park. There are a total of 79 oceanside and bayside drive-in sites, each with a picnic table and fire ring. Camping fee is $30 per night. Drinking water, chemical toilets, cold water showers, and a dump station is available. Pets are welcome. There is a 14-day length of stay limit. Reservations are accepted and can be made online at recreation.gov or by calling 877-444-6777. From mid-November to mid-March, campsites are only available on a first-come, first-served basis.

PARK DETAILS

Catoctin Mountain Park

6602 Foxville Rd
Thurmont, MD 21788
Phone: 301-663-9388

Description
Originally established in 1936 as the Catoctin Recreational Demonstration Area, the 5,810-acre park was intended to provide recreational camps for employee groups. One of the camps eventually became the home of Presidential retreat, Camp David. Although Camp David is not open or accessible to the public, the eastern hardwood forest of Catoctin Mountain Park offers a variety of outdoor opportunities for visitors.

Information
Information is available from the visitor center located on Park Central Road about four miles west of Thurmont via SR-77. The center is open all year except Thanksgiving, Christmas, and New Year's Day. A small exhibit area features native wildlife and cultural history. Parking at the visitor center can be a challenge on busy weekends. Parking along SR-77 is legal as long as your vehicle is entirely outside the white line.

Fees & Season
The park is open all year but there may be temporary road closures from December through March. No entrance fee is charged.

Directions
Catoctin Mountain Park is in northern Maryland about 20 miles east of Hagerstown. The park lies west of US-15 in Thurmont and is accessible from SR-77.

RV CAMPING

Owens Creek Campground
Located on Foxville Deerfield Road about two miles north of SR-77. Open May to mid-November, 50 sites with picnic tables and grills, $30 per night, drinking water, restrooms with flush toilets, showers. Pets welcome. The campground can accommodate RVs up to 22 feet long. There is a 14-day stay limit. Reservations

are accepted and can be made online at recreation.gov or by calling 877-444-6777.

PARK DETAILS

Chesapeake & Ohio Canal National Historical Park

1850 Dual Hwy, Ste 100
Hagerstown, MD 21740
Phone: 301-739-4200

Description
The park follows the route of the Potomac River for 184.5 miles from Washington, D.C. to Cumberland, Maryland. Hundreds of original structures including locks, lockhouses, and aqueducts are among the park's features. The canal operated for nearly 100 years transporting coal, lumber, and agricultural products. The historical park receives nearly five million visitors annually.

Information
Six visitor centers are located throughout the park. The Brunswick Visitor Center is located at 40 West Potomac Street in Brunswick. Cumberland Visitor Center is in Cumberland at 13 Canal Street. Georgetown Visitor Center is in Washington, D.C. at 1057 Thomas Jefferson Street NW. The Great Falls Tavern Visitor Center is at 11710 MacArthur Boulevard in Potomac, Maryland. Hancock Visitor Center is in Hancock, Maryland, at 326 East Main Street. Williamsport Visitor Center is located at 205 West Potomac Street in Williamsport, Maryland. All have some type of exhibit on the canal's history as well as brochures. Only the Great Falls Tavern and Cumberland visitor centers operate year-round, other visitor centers operate on a seasonal schedule. All facilities are closed Thanksgiving Day, Christmas Day, and New Year's Day.

Fees & Season
The park is open all year. An entrance fee of $15 is charged only at the Great Falls entrance. The entrance pass is valid for three days. All other access to the park is free.

Directions

Chesapeake and Ohio Canal National Historical Park runs through central Maryland. Portions also extend into the District of Columbia and West Virginia.

RV CAMPING

Fifteen Mile Creek Campground

Located near Little Orleans, east of Cumberland and about six miles south of I-68 Exit 68. RVers should use High Germany Road to get to the campground as there is a tunnel just before the campground entrance from Orleans Road. Open all year, nine sites with picnic tables and grills, $20 per night, drinking water, pit toilets. The campground can accommodate RVs up to 20 feet long. There is a 14-day length of stay limit. Reservations are required and can be made online at recreation.gov or by calling 877-444-6777.

McCoys Ferry Campground

Located west of Hagerstown about four miles south of I-70 Exit 12. Open all year, 12 sites with picnic tables and grills, $20 per night, drinking water, pit toilets. The campground can accommodate RVs up to 20 feet long. There is an RV height restriction of 7 feet 8 inches at this campground; a tunnel is located just before the campground entrance. There is a 14-day length of stay limit. Reservations are required and can be made online at recreation.gov or by calling 877-444-6777.

Spring Gap Campground

Located eight miles south of Cumberland via SR-51. Open all year, 12 sites with picnic tables and grills, $20 per night, drinking water, pit toilets. The campground can accommodate RVs up to 20 feet long at some sites. There is a 14-day length of stay limit. Reservations are required and can be made online at recreation.gov or by calling 877-444-6777.

PARK DETAILS

Greenbelt Park

6565 Greenbelt Rd
Greenbelt, MD 20770
Phone: 301-344-3944

Description

Established in 1950, the park protects more than 1,100 acres of woodland inhabited by white-tailed deer, red foxes, a variety of birds, and other wildlife. The park features more than nine miles of trails and three picnic areas. Located inside the I-495 loop around Washington, D.C., the park provides a wilderness escape from the noises of the city.

Information

Information is available from the park headquarters located near the park's entrance. The office is open weekdays from 8am to 3:45pm. Information is also available from the ranger station located near the campground entrance. The ranger station is open from 8am to 3:45pm. Both locations are closed on Thanksgiving, Christmas, and New Year's Day.

Fees & Season

The park typically remains open year-round. No entrance fee is charged.

Directions

Greenbelt Park is located 12 miles northeast of Washington, D.C. The park's entrance is accessible from I-95/I-495 Exit 23 via SR-201 and Greenbelt Rd.

RV CAMPING

Greenbelt Park Campground

Located along Park Central Road about 1.5 miles from the park entrance. Open all year, 98 sites with picnic tables and fire rings, $20 per night, drinking water, restrooms with flush toilets, showers, dump station. Pets welcome. The campground can accommodate RVs up to 36 feet. There is a 14-day stay limit. Reservations are required and can be made online at recreation.gov or by calling 877-444-6777.

Michigan

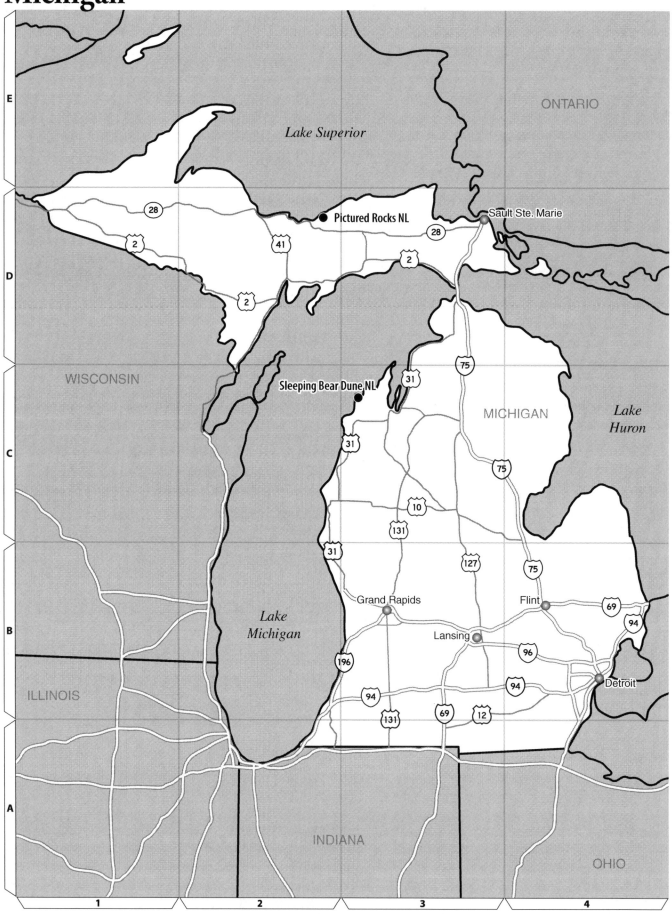

ONTARIO

Lake Superior

28

Pictured Rocks NL

Sault Ste. Marie

41

28

2

2

WISCONSIN

2

31

75

Sleeping Bear Dune NL

31

MICHIGAN

Lake Huron

31

10

131

127

75

Grand Rapids

Flint

75

69

Lake Michigan

94

B

Lansing

96

196

Detroit

ILLINOIS

94

94

131

69

12

INDIANA

OHIO

1 2 3 4

Michigan Parks

	Map	Auto Touring	Biking	Boating	Climbing	Fishing	Hiking	Horseback Riding	Hunting	Snow Skiing	Swimming	Visitor Center	Wildlife Viewing
Pictured Rocks National Lakeshore	D2			•		•	•		•			•	•
Sleeping Bear Dunes National Lakeshore	C3	•		•		•	•		•		•	•	•

PARK DETAILS

Pictured Rocks National Lakeshore

PO Box 40
Munising, MI 49862
Phone: 906-387-3700

Description
Pictured Rocks National Lakeshore was authorized in 1966 and encompasses 73,235 acres. Features include sandstone cliffs, long beach strands, sand dunes, waterfalls, inland lakes, wetlands, and hardwood forests. The park also features historic sites such as an 1874 lighthouse, early U.S. Coast Guard lifeboat stations, old farmsteads, and a Civil War era iron blast furnace site.

Information
Information is available from the Munising Falls Visitor Center located at 1505 Sand Point Road in Munising. The visitor center is open daily in summer between 9am and 5pm. It features paved trails to several overlooks, wayside exhibits, and access to the North Country National Scenic Trail.

Information is also available from the Grand Sable Visitor Center, located on County Road H-58 about one mile west of Grand Marais. The visitor center is open daily in summer between 9am and 5pm. The North Country National Scenic Trail can be accessed from here.

Fees & Season
The park remains open all year but many roads are closed by snow in winter. No entrance fee is charged.

Directions
Pictured Rocks National Lakeshore is in northern Michigan between Munising and Grand Marais. There are numerous access points along County Road H-58.

RV CAMPING

Hurricane River Campground
Located 12 miles west of Grand Marais on County Road H-58 on the shores of Lake Superior. Open mid-May through October, 21 sites with picnic tables and fire grates, $14 per night, water, pit toilets. Pets welcome. There is a 14-day stay limit. The campground can accommodate RVs up to 36 feet (42 feet vehicle/ trailer combination). Sites are available on a first-come, first-served basis; reservations are not accepted. The campground fills up quickly on weekends and all of July and August; an early morning arrival is suggested.

Little Beaver Lake Campground
Located 20 miles northeast of Munising off County Road H-58. Open mid-May through October, eight sites with picnic tables and fire grates, $14 per night, water, pit toilets, nature trail, boat ramp. Pets welcome. There is a 14 day maximum stay limit. Single unit vehicles in excess of 36 feet and vehicle/trailer combined units in excess of 42 feet are prohibited because of the small campsites and the narrow, twisting, hilly access road. Sites are available on a first-come, first-served basis; reservations are not accepted. The campground fills up quickly on weekends and all of July and August; an early morning arrival is suggested.

Twelvemile Beach Campground
Located 15 miles west of Grand Marais off County Road H-58. Open mid-May through October, 36 sites with picnic tables and fire grates, $14 per night (lakeside sites are $16 per night), water, pit toilets, nature trail. Pets welcome. There is a 14 day stay limit. Because the turning radius and some parking site lengths are limited within the campground, single unit vehicles

in excess of 36 feet and vehicle/trailer combined units in excess of 42 feet are not recommended. Sites are available on a first-come, first-served basis; reservations are not accepted. The campground fills up quickly on weekends and all of July and August; an early morning arrival is suggested.

PARK DETAILS

Sleeping Bear Dunes National Lakeshore

9922 Front St
Empire, MI 49630
Phone: 231-326-4700

Description

Sleeping Bear Dunes National Lakeshore encompasses a 35-mile stretch of Lake Michigan's eastern coastline. The park was established in 1977 and features hardwood forests, beaches, sand dunes, and steep bluffs. Nearly two million visitors come to the park every year.

Scenic Drives

The Pierce Stocking Scenic Drive is a 7.4 mile self-guided auto tour. There are 12 numbered interpretive stops along the route. The loop drive is accessed from SR-109 about 3.5 miles north of Empire. The scenic drive provides the visitor with insight to the history of the area and scenic overlooks of Glen Lake, Sleeping Bear Dunes and Lake Michigan.

Information

Information is available from the Philip A. Hart Visitor Center located on highway M-72 in Empire. The center is open all year except Thanksgiving, Christmas, and New Year's Day. Summer hours are 8am to 6pm and 8:30am to 4pm in fall, winter, and spring. Exhibits describe the geologic, natural history, and human stories of the park. Information is also available from ranger stations in both campgrounds.

Fees & Season

The park remains open year-round. An entrance fee of $25 is charged and is valid for seven days.

Directions

Sleeping Bear Dunes National Lakeshore is in central Michigan about 24 miles west of Traverse City. There are numerous park access points along SR-22.

RV CAMPING

D.H. Day Campground

Located two miles west of Glen Arbor off SR-109. Open April through November, 88 sites with picnic tables and fire rings, $20 per night, potable water, vault toilets, dump station, amphitheater. Pets welcome. There is a 14-day stay limit. Sites are available on a first-come, first-served basis; reservations are not accepted.

Platte River Campground

Located ten miles south of Empire on Lake Michigan Road off SR-22. Open all year, 96 sites with 30-amp electric hookups ($31 per night), 53 sites without hookups ($26 per night), picnic tables, fire rings, water, restrooms with flush toilets, hot showers, dump station, amphitheater. Some pull-through sites are available. Pets welcome. There is a 14-day stay limit. Reservations are accepted and can be made online at recreation.gov or by calling 877-444-6777.

Mississippi

TENNESSEE

E

78

45

61

Sardis

278

Tupelo

278

55

45

ARKANSAS

D

61

82

82

45

Natchez Trace Pkwy

MISSISSIPPI

45

C

Meridian

20

Jackson

20

LOUISIANA

61

ALABAMA

49

55

45

84

59

Natchez

84

B

61

Hattiesburg

98

49

10

A

■ *Gulf Islands NS (see Florida)*

Gulf of Mexico

1   2   3   4

Mississippi Parks

	Map	Auto Touring	Biking	Boating	Climbing	Fishing	Hiking	Horseback Riding	Hunting	Snow Skiing	Swimming	Visitor Center	Wildlife Viewing
Gulf Islands National Seashore - *see Florida*	A4		•	•		•	•		•			•	•
Natchez Trace Parkway	C3	•	•	•		•	•		•			•	•

PARK DETAILS

Natchez Trace Parkway

2680 Natchez Trace Parkway
Tupelo, MS 38804
Phone: 800-305-7417

Description

Natchez Trace Parkway is a 444-mile route across Mississippi, Alabama, and Tennessee. It generally follows the trail used by American Indians and early settlers. The parkway was established in 1938. RVers planning to drive the route need to know there is a length restriction of 55 feet, including tow vehicle, and a height restriction of 14 feet.

Information

Information is available from the visitor center in Tupelo at Milepost 266. The visitor center is open daily between 9am and 4:30pm; it closes on Thanksgiving, Christmas, and New Year's Day. Several remote contact stations are located along the parkway.

Fees & Season

The Parkway is generally open year-round but may occasionally close during hazardous weather. There is no entrance fee.

Directions

The Parkway travels between Natchez, Mississippi, and Nashville, Tennessee. There are numerous access points including major highways such as Interstate 20 near Clinton, Mississippi; Interstate 55 in Jackson, Mississippi; and Interstate 40 west of Nashville, Tennessee.

RV CAMPING

Jeff Busby Campground

Located in Mississippi at milepost 193.1 about 12 miles south of Mathiston. Open all year, 18 sites with picnic tables, drinking water, restrooms, nature trail, public phone. No camping fee is charged. There is a 14-day stay limit. All sites are available on a first-come, first-served basis; reservations are not accepted.

Meriwether Lewis Campground

Located in Tennessee at milepost 385.9 about seven miles east of Hohenwald. Open all year, 32 sites with picnic tables, drinking water, restrooms, nature trails. No camping fee is charged. There is a 14-day length of stay limit. All sites are available on a first-come, first-served basis; reservations are not accepted.

Rocky Springs Campground

Located in Mississippi at milepost 54.8 about 15 miles northeast of Port Gibson. Open all year, 22 sites with picnic tables, drinking water, restrooms, nature trails, public phone. No camping fee is charged. There is a 14-day length of stay limit. All sites are available on a first-come, first-served basis; reservations are not accepted.

Missouri

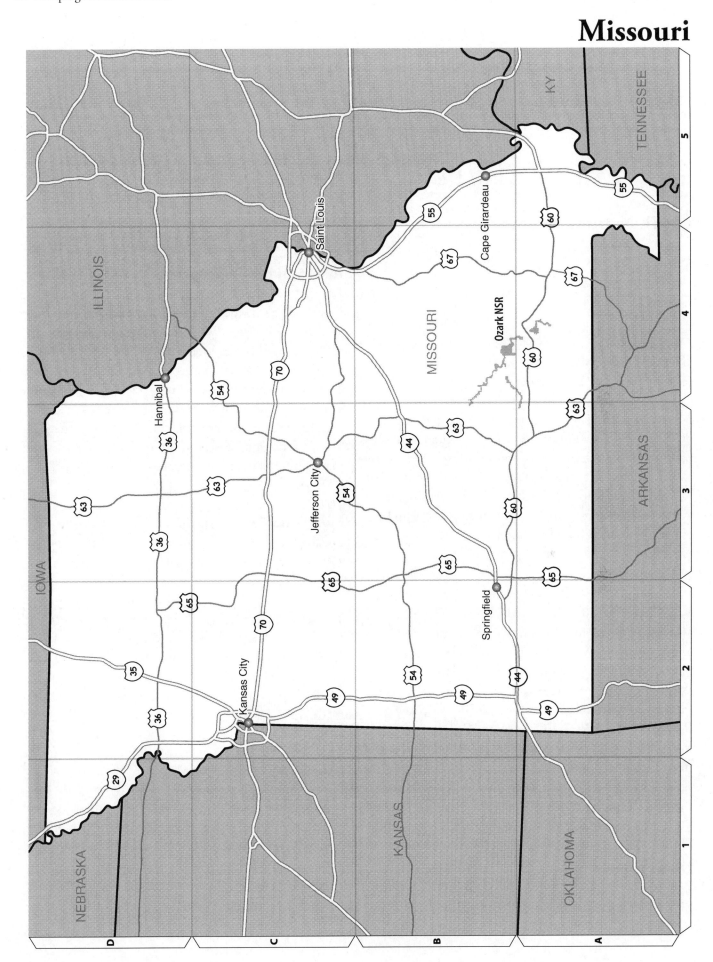

Missouri Parks

Map	Auto Touring	Biking	Boating	Climbing	Fishing	Hiking	Horseback Riding	Hunting	Snow Skiing	Swimming	Visitor Center	Wildlife Viewing
Ozark National Scenic Riverways	B4	•	•	•		•	•	•	•			•	•	•

PARK DETAILS

Ozark National Scenic Riverways

PO Box 490
Van Buren, MO 63965
Phone: 573-323-4236

Description

Ozark National Scenic Riverways is the first national park to protect a river system. The park protects 134 miles of the Current and Jacks Fork rivers in southeast Missouri. Established in 1964, the park encompasses 80,790 acres. In addition to protecting the rivers, the park is home to hundreds of freshwater springs, caves, trails, and historic sites such as Alley Mill, which was built in 1894. About 1.5 million people visit the park every year. Visitation is heaviest during the summer, especially weekends and holidays.

Information

Information can be obtained from park headquarters in Van Buren. The office is located just east of town at 404 Watercress Drive and is open year-round on weekdays, and daily from Memorial Day to Labor Day, from 8am to 4:30pm (closed on holidays). Features include exhibits on the resources and history of the Ozarks, informational brochures, and books. Alley Spring and Round Spring Visitor Information Centers are open from Memorial Day to Labor Day, seven days a week from 8am to 4:30pm.

Fees & Season

The park is open year-round. There is no entrance fee.

Directions

The park is accessible from various points along US-60, SR-17, SR-19, and SR-106. Main roads throughout the park are well maintained state highways but are hilly and winding. Roads leading into the backcountry areas are typically dirt and less maintained.

RV CAMPING

Alley Spring Campground

Located six miles west of Eminence along SR-106. Open all year, peak season is mid-April through October, 146 sites with picnic tables and fire rings ($19 per night), 26 sites with water and 20/30/50-amp electric service ($22 per night), restrooms with flush toilets, hot showers, dump station. Pets welcome. During the off-season, camping fees are reduced as are some services such as availability of water. There is a 14-day stay limit. Reservations are accepted and can be made online at recreation.gov or by calling 877-444-6777.

Big Spring Campground

Located four miles south of Van Buren along SR-103. Open all year, peak season is mid-April through October, 100 sites with picnic tables and fire rings ($19 per night), 28 sites with water and 20/30/50-amp electric service ($22 per night), restrooms with flush toilets, hot showers, dump station. Pets welcome. During the off-season, camping fees are reduced as are some services such as availability of water. There is a 14-day stay limit. Reservations are accepted and can be made online at recreation.gov or by calling 877-444-6777.

Powder Mill Campground

Located 14 miles east of Eminence via SR-106. Open all year, 10 sites with picnic tables and fire rings, $19 per night. Pets welcome. There is a 14-day stay limit. Sites are available on a first-come, first-served basis only; reservations are not accepted. *Campground is currently closed due to flood damage.*

Pulltite Campground

Located 24 miles north of Eminence via SR-19 and SR-EE. Open all year, peak season is mid-April through October, 55 sites with picnic tables and fire rings, $19 per night, restrooms with flush toilets, hot showers. Pets welcome. During the off-season, camping fees are reduced as are some services such as availability of water. There is a 14-day stay limit. Reservations are accepted and can be made online at recreation.gov or by calling 877-444-6777.

Round Spring Campground

Located 16 miles north of Eminence along SR-19. Open all year, peak season is mid-April through October, 46 sites with picnic tables and fire rings ($19 per night), six sites with water and 20/30/50-amp electric service ($22 per night), restrooms with flush toilets, hot showers, dump station. Pets welcome. During the off-season, camping fees are reduced as are some services such as availability of water. There is a 14-day stay limit. Reservations are accepted and can be made online at recreation.gov or by calling 877-444-6777. Round Spring Cave is nearby.

Two Rivers Campground

Located seven miles east of Eminence via SR-106 and SR-V. Open all year, peak season is mid-April through October, 22 sites with picnic tables and fire rings, $19 per night, restrooms with flush toilets, hot showers. Pets welcome. During the off-season, camping fees are reduced as are some services such as availability of water. There is a 14-day stay limit. Reservations are accepted and can be made online at recreation.gov or by calling 877-444-6777.

Montana

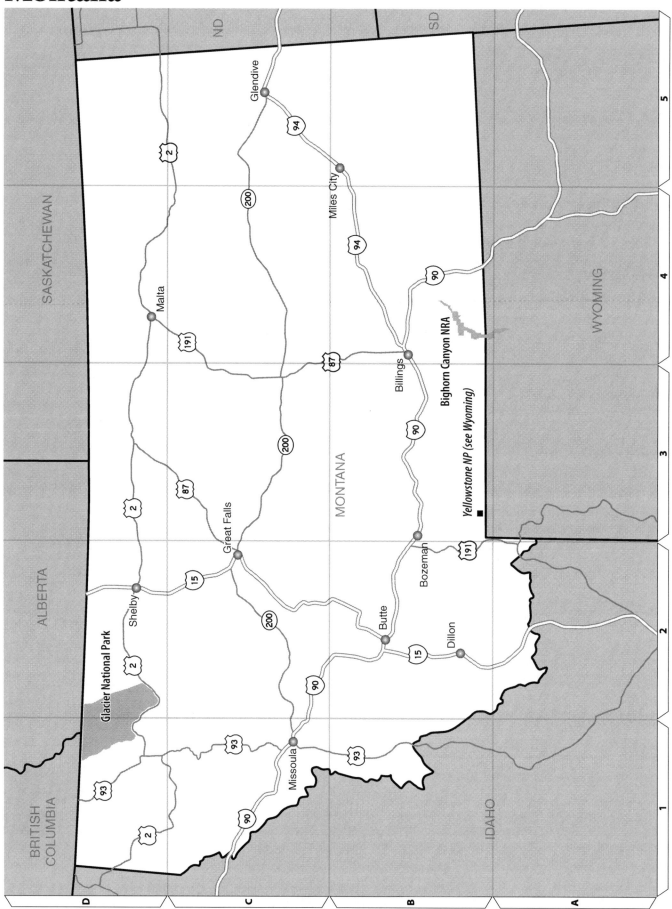

Montana Parks

	Map	Auto Touring	Biking	Boating	Climbing	Fishing	Hiking	Horseback Riding	Hunting	Snow Skiing	Swimming	Visitor Center	Wildlife Viewing
Bighorn Canyon National Recreation Area	B4	•	•	•		•	•		•			•	•
Glacier National Park	D2	•	•	•		•	•	•				•	•
Yellowstone National Park - *see Wyoming*	B3	•	•	•		•	•	•			•		•

PARK DETAILS

Bighorn Canyon National Recreation Area

PO Box 7458
Fort Smith, MT 59035
Phone: 307-548-5406

Description

Bighorn Canyon National Recreation Area was established in 1966 and protects over 120,000 acres of land surrounding the Bighorn River. There are two districts to the park; the north lies in Montana, the south in Wyoming. The north and south districts are not connected to each other by road. Most visitors come to this park for the boating and fishing opportunities but the park does have 14 hiking trails and four historic ranches worth seeing.

Information

Information is available from two visitor centers and two contact stations. The Bighorn Canyon Visitor Center in Lovell, Wyoming, is open daily all year and features a relief map of Bighorn Canyon, films, restrooms, picnic area, nature trail, and a bookstore. It closes on Thanksgiving, Christmas, and New Year's Day. The Yellowtail Dam Visitor Center is near Fort Smith, Montana, and is open Memorial Day to Labor Day. A variety of films shown upon request are available.

Within the southern district of the park along SR-37 is the Crooked Creek Contact Station. It is staffed when possible and has information about four historic ranches within the recreation area. The Afterbay Contact Station is in Fort Smith, Montana, and is also open when staffing allows. Two films are available for viewing upon request.

Fees & Season

The park remains open year-round. No entrance fee is charged.

Directions

Bighorn Canyon National Recreation Area is in south-central Montana and northern Wyoming. The northern portion of the park is accessed from I-90 Exit 495 in Hardin, Montana, by following SR-313 south for 43 miles. The southern portion of the park lies to the north of US-14A in Wyoming.

RV CAMPING

Afterbay Campground

Located about 42 miles south of Hardin, Montana, off SR-313. Open all year, 28 sites with picnic tables and grills, $10 per night, potable water, vault toilets, dump station. Pets welcome. There is a 14-day stay limit. All sites are available on a first-come, first-served basis; reservations are not accepted. An additional 12 sites without water are available on the north shore of Afterbay.

Horseshoe Bend Campground

Located about 14 miles north of Lovell, Wyoming, via SR-37. Open all year, 48 sites with picnic tables and grills (19 with water and electric service), $10 per night for sites without utilities, $25 per night for sites with utilities, drinking water, restrooms with flush toilets, dump station. The campground can accommodate large RVs. Utilities are turned off between September and May. Pets welcome. There is a 14-day stay limit. All sites are available on a first-come, first-served basis;

reservations are not accepted. The campground is managed by a concessionaire.

Trail Creek Campground

Located along Barry's Landing Road about 27 miles north of Lovell, Wyoming, via SR-37. Open all year, 14 sites with picnic tables and grills, $10 per night, vault toilets. Ten sites are for smaller RVs, four sites located just off Barry's Landing parking lot can accommodate larger RVs. Pets welcome. There is a 14-day stay limit. All sites are available on a first-come, first-served basis; reservations are not accepted. The campground is managed by a concessionaire.

PARK DETAILS

Glacier National Park

PO Box 128
West Glacier, MT 59936
Phone: 406-888-7800

Description

Glacier National Park was established in 1910 and preserves over one million acres of forests, alpine meadows, rugged mountains, and beautiful lakes. The park features over 700 miles of trails and the scenic Going-to-the-Sun Road, which crosses the park and provides some spectacular views. Around two million visitors come to the park every year, mostly during the warmer months.

Scenic Drives

Going-to-the-Sun Road is a 50-mile paved route across the park. The road is narrow, winding, and steep at times; there are vehicle length and width restrictions in place. Numerous scenic turnouts along the route offer spectacular views into the park's mountainous landscape. Vehicles, and vehicle combinations, longer than 21 feet (including bumpers) or wider than 8 feet (including mirrors), are prohibited between Avalanche and Rising Sun campgrounds. Vehicles over 10 feet in height may have difficulty driving west from Logan Pass, due to rock overhangs.

Information

Information is available from three visitor centers. The Apgar Visitor Center, located just inside the park off US-2 at West Glacier, is open year-round but hours vary by season. Logan Pass Visitor Center is located along the Going-to-the-Sun Road; its opening and closing dates depend on weather conditions and when the road is open. The Saint Mary Visitor Center is off US-89 and is open daily from late May to late September; hours vary.

Fees & Season

The park is open year-round but some visitor facilities close during winter; generally from late May to early September all facilities are open. An entrance fee is charged that is valid for seven days. From May through October the fee is $35; November through April, $25.

Directions

Glacier National Park is in northwest Montana about 140 miles north of Missoula. The park is accessible from points along US-2 and US-89.

RV CAMPING

Apgar Campground

Located two miles north of West Glacier near the Apgar Visitor Center. Open May to early October, 194 sites, $20 per night, drinking water, restrooms with flush toilets, dump station. Pets welcome. The campground can accommodate RVs up to 40 feet long at 25 sites. There is a 14-day stay limit in July and August; 30 days the rest of the season. All sites are available on a first-come, first-served basis; reservations are not accepted.

Avalanche Campground

Located along the Going-to-the-Sun Road about 15 miles northeast of West Glacier. Open mid-June to early September, 87 sites, $20 per night, drinking water, restrooms with flush toilets. Pets welcome. The campground can accommodate RVs up to 26 feet at 50 sites. There is a 14-day stay limit in July and August; 30 days the rest of the season. All sites are available on a first-come, first-served basis; reservations are not accepted.

Fish Creek Campground

Located four miles north of West Glacier via Camas Road. Open June to early September, 178 sites, $23 per night, drinking water, restrooms with flush toilets, coin-operated showers, dump station. Pets welcome. The campground can accommodate RVs up to 35 feet at 18 sites. There is a 14-day stay limit in July and August; 30 days the rest of the season. Reservations are accepted and can be made online at recreation.gov or by calling 877-444-6777.

Many Glacier Campground

Located 12 miles west of Babb on Many Glacier Road. Open May to late September, 109 sites, $23 per night, drinking water, restrooms with flush toilets, dump station. Pets welcome. The campground can accommodate RVs up to 35 feet at 13 sites. There is a 14-day stay limit in July and August; 30 days the rest of the season. Reservations are accepted and can be made online at recreation.gov or by calling 877-444-6777.

Rising Sun Campground

Located six miles west of Saint Mary along Going-to-the-Sun Road. Open June to September, 84 sites, $20 per night, drinking water, restrooms with flush toilets, dump station. Pets welcome. The campground can accommodate RVs up to 25 feet at 10 sites. There is a 14-day stay limit in July and August; 30 days the rest of the season. All sites are available on a first-come, first-served basis; reservations are not accepted.

Saint Mary Campground

Located just west of US-89 at Saint Mary along Going-to-the-Sun Road. Open April through October, 148 sites, $23 per night, drinking water, restrooms with flush toilets, dump station. Pets welcome. The campground can accommodate RVs up to 40 feet at three sites and 35 feet at 22 sites. There is a 14-day stay limit in July and August; 30 days the rest of the season. Reservations are accepted and can be made online at recreation.gov or by calling 877-444-6777.

Two Medicine Campground

Located 13 miles northwest of East Glacier Park via SR-49. Open late May to late September, 100 sites, $20 per night, drinking water, restrooms with flush toilets, dump station. Pets welcome. The campground can accommodate RVs up to 35 feet at 10 sites. There is a 14-day stay limit in July and August; 30 days the rest of the season. All sites are available on a first-come, first-served basis; reservations are not accepted.

Nevada

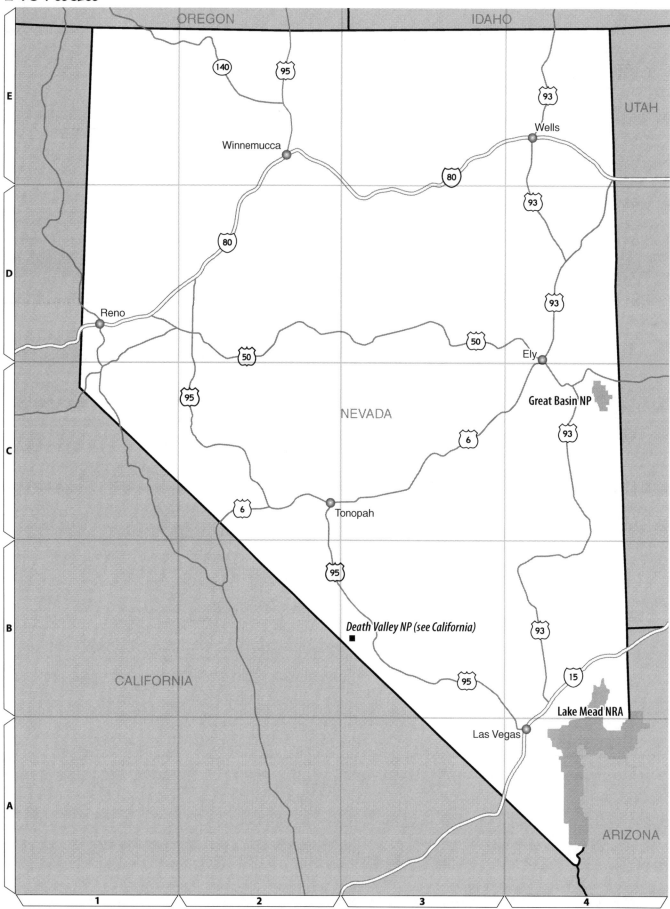

Nevada Parks

	Map	Auto Touring	Biking	Boating	Climbing	Fishing	Hiking	Horseback Riding	Hunting	Snow Skiing	Swimming	Visitor Center	Wildlife Viewing
Death Valley National Park - *see California*	B3	•	•				•		•		•	•	•
Great Basin National Park	C4	•	•			•	•		•			•	•
Lake Mead National Recreation Area	A4	•	•	•		•	•	•	•		•	•	•

PARK DETAILS

Great Basin National Park

100 Great Basin National Park
Baker, NV 89311
Phone: 775-234-7331

Description

Great Basin National Park features 13,063-foot Wheeler Peak, 5,000 year old bristlecone pine trees, and numerous limestone caverns, including Lehman Caves. The park was established in 1986 and encompasses 77,180 acres of land, streams, lakes, and mountain peaks. Two different guided tours of Lehman Caves are offered daily, year-round. Reservations are strongly recommended in summer and holiday weekends. The park receives over 150,000 visitors every year. It is one of few designated an International Dark-Sky Park.

Scenic Drives

Wheeler Peak Scenic Drive is a 12-mile, paved but steep and winding road with an average grade of 8 percent. The scenic route beyond Upper Lehman Creek Campground is closed to single vehicles or trailers in excess of 24 feet. The road to Upper Lehman Creek Campground is open year-round; the upper nine miles beyond the campground are generally open June through October, depending on weather.

Information

Information is available from the Great Basin Visitor Center, located just north of the town of Baker on the west side of SR-487. The visitor center is open daily in summer from 8am to 5:30pm. It has an information desk, exhibits, theater with orientation film, and brochures. Information is also available year-round at the Lehman Caves Visitor Center, which is in the park about five miles west of Baker. Hours are 8am to 5pm in summer and 8am to 4:30pm fall through spring; it closes on Thanksgiving, Christmas, and New Year's Day. Tickets for cave tours are sold here. It also has an information desk, exhibits, theater with orientation film, and brochures.

Fees & Season

The park remains open year-round but road closures occur in winter. There is no entrance fee charged. There is a per person fee charged for cave tours. A fee is charged for use of the dump station, which is located 1/2 mile inside the park and usually open late May to October.

Directions

Great Basin National Park is in east-central Nevada about 60 miles east of Ely. From Ely, go east on US-6/US-50 about 56 miles then follow SR-487 south 5 miles to Baker and go west on SR-488 into the park.

RV CAMPING

Baker Creek Campground

Located three miles from the park's entrance on Baker Creek Road. Open May to October, 38 sites with picnic tables and grills, some pull-through sites, $15 per night, drinking water in summer, vault toilets. Pets welcome. The campground can accommodate large RVs at some sites. There is a 14-day stay limit. Campsites are available on a first-come, first-served basis; reservations are not accepted.

Lower Lehman Creek Campground

Located on Wheeler Peak Scenic Drive about 2.5 miles from the Lehman Caves Visitor Center. Open year-round, 11 sites with picnic tables and grills, some pull-through sites, $15 per night, drinking water in summer, vault toilets. Pets welcome. The campground can accommodate large RVs at some sites. There is a 14-day stay limit. Campsites are available on a first-come, first-served basis; reservations are not accepted.

Upper Lehman Creek Campground

Located on Wheeler Peak Scenic Drive about 3.5 miles from the Lehman Caves Visitor Center. Open mid-April to October, 24 sites with picnic tables and grills, $15 per night, drinking water in summer, vault toilets. Pets welcome. The campground can accommodate large RVs at some sites. There is a 14-day stay limit. Campsites are available on a first-come, first-served basis; reservations are not accepted.

PARK DETAILS

Lake Mead National Recreation Area

601 Nevada Way
Boulder City, NV 89005
Phone: 702-293-8990

Description

Lake Mead National Recreation Area offers year-round recreational opportunities for boating, fishing, hiking, photography, picnicking, and sightseeing. Established in 1964, the recreation area encompasses nearly 1.5 million acres of mountains and desert landscape. The park straddles the Arizona/Nevada state line and receives nearly eight million visitors every year.

Information

Information is available from the Alan Bible Visitor Center off US-93 about four miles east of Boulder City, Nevada. The visitor center features a relief map of the recreation area, geology exhibit, gift store, orientation film, and brochures. It is open daily from 9am to 4:30pm except on Thanksgiving, Christmas, and New Year's Day.

Fees & Season

The park is open all year. An entrance fee of $25 per vehicle is charged and is valid for seven days.

Directions

Lake Mead National Recreation Area is in southeast Nevada and northwest Arizona. There are numerous access points into the park from US-93, US-95 and SR-167.

RV CAMPING

Boulder Beach Campground

Located two miles north of the visitor center along Lakeshore Road. Open all year, 146 sites with picnic tables and grills, $20 per night, drinking water, restrooms with flush toilets, dump station. Fee based WiFi available. Pets welcome. There is a 30-day stay limit. Sites are available on a first-come, first-served basis; reservations are not accepted.

Boulder Beach RV Park

Located along Lakeshore Road about two miles north of the visitor center, adjacent to the Boulder Beach Campground. Concessionaire-operated campground. Open all year, 115 sites with full hookups, $34 to $50 per night, some pull-thru sites, coin laundry, propane sales, convenience store. Fee based WiFi available. Reservations are accepted and can be made online at lakemeadrvvillage.com or by calling 702-293-2540.

Callville Bay Campground

Located 22 miles northeast of Henderson off SR-167/Northshore Rd. Open all year, 52 sites with picnic tables and grills, $20 per night, drinking water, restrooms with flush toilets, dump station. Fee based WiFi available. Pets welcome. There is a 30-day stay limit. Sites are available on a first-come, first-served basis; reservations are not accepted.

Callville Bay RV Park

Located about 22 miles northeast of Henderson off SR-167/Northshore Rd. Concessionaire-operated campground. Open all year, five RV sites with full hookups, $20 per night. Reservations may be made by contacting Callville Bay Resorts at 702-565-8958.

Cottonwood Cove Campground

On Lake Mohave about 14 miles east of Searchlight. Open all year, 145 sites with picnic tables and grills, $20 per night, drinking water, restrooms with flush toilets, dump station. Fee based WiFi available. Pets welcome. There is a 30-day stay limit. Sites are available on a first-come, first-served basis; reservations are not accepted.

Cottonwood Cove RV Park

On Lake Mohave about 14 miles east of Searchlight. Concessionaire-operated campground. Open all year, 72 sites with full hookups, $41 to $50 per night in summer, $35 to $45 in winter, coin laundry, restrooms with flush toilets. Fee based WiFi available. Reservations are accepted and can be made online at cottonwoodcoveresort.com or by calling 800-255-5561.

Echo Bay Campground

Located 30 miles south of Moapa Valley/Overton off SR-167/Northshore Rd. Open all year, 166 sites with picnic tables and grills, $20 per night, drinking water, restrooms with flush toilets, dump station. Pets welcome. There is a 30-day stay limit. Sites are available on a first-come, first-served basis; reservations are not accepted.

Echo Bay RV Park

Located 30 miles south of Moapa Valley/Overton off SR-167/Northshore Rd. Concession operated campground. Open all year, 55 RV sites with full hookups, restrooms with flush toilets, showers, coin laundry, convenience store, gas and propane sales. Fee based WiFi available. Reservations are accepted and can be made online at lakemeadrvvillage.com or by calling 702-293-2540.

Katherine Landing Campground

On Lake Mohave in Arizona about five miles north of Bullhead City via SR-68 and Davis Dam Road. Concession operated campground. Open all year, 173 sites with picnic tables and grills, $20 per night, drinking water, restrooms with flush toilets, dump station. Fee based WiFi available. Pets welcome. There is a 30-day stay limit. Sites are available on a first-come, first-served basis; reservations are not accepted.

Katherine Landing RV Park

On Lake Mohave in Arizona about five miles north of Bullhead City via SR-68 and Davis Dam Road. Concession operated campground. Open all year, 25 RV sites with full hookups, $35 per night, restrooms with flush toilets, showers, coin laundry. Fee based WiFi available. Reservations may be made by contacting Katherine Landing Recreation Company at 928-754-3245.

Las Vegas Bay Campground

Located eight miles northeast of Henderson off SR-167/Northshore Rd. Open all year, 85 sites with picnic tables and grills, $20 per night, drinking water, restrooms with flush toilets, dump station. Fee based WiFi available. Pets welcome. There is a 30-day stay limit. Sites are available on a first-come, first-served basis; reservations are not accepted.

Temple Bar Campground

In Arizona about 80 miles north of Kingman via US-93. Open all year, 153 sites with picnic tables and grills, $20 per night, drinking water, restrooms with flush toilets, dump station. Fee based WiFi available. Pets welcome. There is a 30-day stay limit. Sites are available on a first-come, first-served basis; reservations are not accepted.

Temple Bar RV Park

In Arizona about 80 miles north of Kingman via US-93. Concession operated campground. Open all year, 10 RV sites with full hookups, $35 per night in summer, $30 per night fall through spring, restrooms with flush toilets, coin operated showers, coin laundry, convenience store, cafe. Fee based WiFi available. Reservations are accepted and may be made online at templebarlakemead.com or by calling 800-255-5561.

Willow Beach Campground

In Arizona on Lake Mohave about 60 miles north of Kingman via US-93. Concession operated campground. Open all year, 28 RV sites with full hookups, $50 per night, drinking water, restrooms with flush toilets, showers, coin laundry, dump station, convenience store, restaurant. Fee based WiFi available. Pets welcome. The campground can accommodate large RVs at some sites. Reservations may be made by contacting Willow Beach at 928-767-4747.

New Mexico

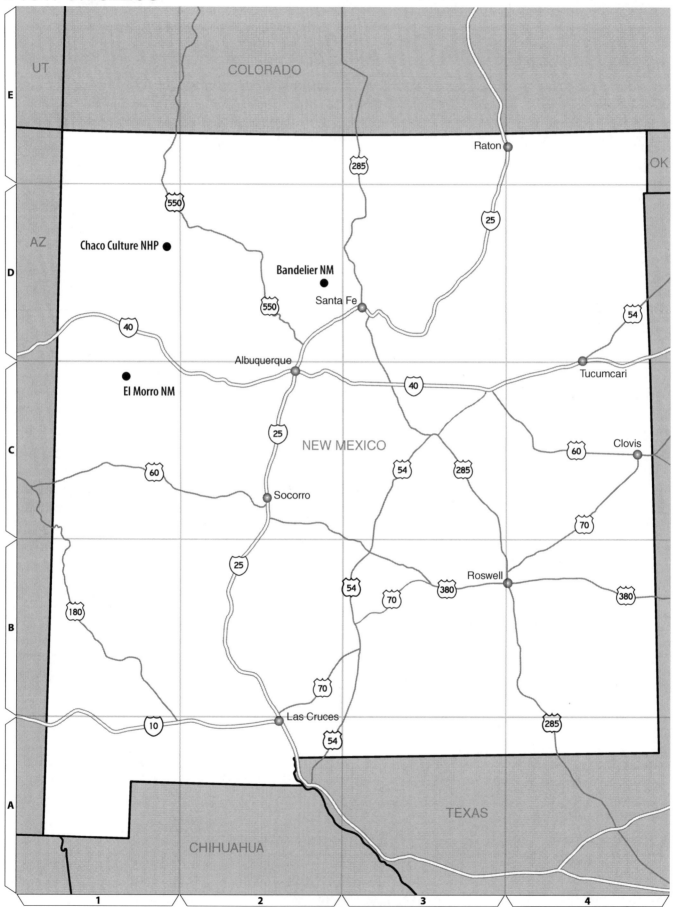

New Mexico Parks

	Map	Auto Touring	Biking	Boating	Climbing	Fishing	Hiking	Horseback Riding	Hunting	Snow Skiing	Swimming	Visitor Center	Wildlife Viewing
Bandelier National Monument	D2						•					•	•
Chaco Culture National Historical Park	D1		•				•					•	•
El Morro National Monument	C1						•					•	•

PARK DETAILS

Bandelier National Monument

15 Entrance Rd
Los Alamos, NM 87544
Phone: 505-672-3861 x517

Description

Bandelier National Monument protects Pueblo Indian cliff houses and villages on mesa tops and canyon walls. The 33,676-acre park was established in 1916. Most of the park is accessible only by trail; there are over 70 miles of trails. If you are planning to only visit the park for the day and not stay in the campground, you're required to take a shuttle bus from the visitor center on SR-4 in White Rock. Buses run every 30 minutes between 9am and 3pm.

Information

Information is available from the visitor center located in Frijoles Canyon, about three miles from the park entrance. The visitor center is open all year except on Christmas and New Year's Day; hours vary depending on season. Features include exhibits of the Pueblo Indian culture. Because of severe space limitations, trailers may not be brought into the parking areas in Frijoles Canyon (drop them off at the campground near the park entrance).

Fees & Season

The park remains open all year except during heavy snow days. An entrance fee of $25 per vehicle is charged and is valid for seven days.

Directions

Bandelier National Monument is in north-central New Mexico about 40 miles west of Santa Fe via US-84, SR-502, and SR-4.

RV CAMPING

Juniper Family Campground

Located near the park's entrance. Open all year, 53 sites with picnic tables and grills, $12 per night, drinking water, restrooms with flush toilets, dump station. Pets welcome. The campground can accommodate RVs up to 40 feet long. It rarely fills to capacity. There is a 14-day stay limit. All sites are available on a first-come, first-served basis; reservations are not accepted. Fees are paid by credit card only at a self-registration kiosk located near the campground entrance. Campers wanting to pay cash will need to do so at the park visitor center during business hours.

PARK DETAILS

Chaco Culture National Historical Park

PO Box 220
Nageezi, NM 87037
Phone: 505-786-7014

Description

Chaco Culture National Historical Park encompasses nearly 34,000 acres and was originally established in 1907 as Chaco Canyon National Monument. The park contains 13 major prehistoric sites and hundreds of smaller ones built by the Ancestral Puebloan people. The park is one of few designated an International

Dark-Sky Park. Night sky programs are typically offered on Friday and Saturday nights from April through October.

Information

Information is available from the park's visitor center located a few miles from the entrance. The visitor center is open daily all year from 8am to 5pm except on Thanksgiving, Christmas, and New Year's Day. A video is shown throughout the day in the auditorium and a museum features exhibits on the cultural history of Chaco Canyon. Books, videos, and gifts are available from the gift shop inside the visitor center.

Fees & Season

The park is open year-round. An entrance fee of $25 per vehicle is charged and is valid for seven days.

Directions

Chaco Culture National Historical Park is in northwest New Mexico about 70 miles southeast of Farmington. The National Park Service recommends not relying on a GPS to access the park as some of the local roads are unsafe for passenger cars. Rather, the National Park Service recommends accessing the park from the north near Nageezi on US-550 at CR 7900. This route is clearly signed from US-550 to the park and includes 8 miles of paved road and 13 miles of rough dirt road. The 4 1/2 miles before entering the park are very rough.

RV CAMPING

Gallo Campground

Located one mile east of the visitor center. Open all year, 35 RV sites with picnic tables and fire grates, $15 per night, restrooms with flush toilets, dump station. Drinking water is available in the visitor center parking area. Pets welcome. The campground can accommodate RVs up to 35 feet. There is a 14-day length of stay limit. Reservations are accepted and can be made online at recreation.gov or by calling 877-444-6777. The campground will occasionally fill up on Friday or Saturday afternoons and on holiday weekends.

PARK DETAILS

El Morro National Monument

HC 61 Box 43
Ramah, NM 87321
Phone: 505-783-4226 x801

Description

Established in 1906, the 1,278-acre monument protects a massive sandstone bluff upon which are carved over two thousand inscriptions and petroglyphs. The bluff was a welcome landmark for weary travelers because of the waterhole hidden at its base. The park also features an Ancestral Puebloan ruin atop the bluff. A picnic area is located near the visitor center.

Information

Information is available from the visitor center located at the end of the park road. The visitor center is usually open daily in summer from 9am to 6pm and 9am to 5pm in fall, winter, and spring. It closes on Thanksgiving, Christmas and New Year's Day. It features an orientation video and museum.

Fees & Season

The park remains open year-round and there is no entrance fee. Portions of the park trail may close during the winter because of ice and snow.

Directions

El Morro National Monument is in west-central New Mexico, 42 miles southwest of Grants via SR-43.

RV CAMPING

El Morro Campground

Located about 1/2 mile from the park's entrance. Open all year, nine sites with picnic tables and grills, water available in summer, pit toilets. Camping is free. Pets welcome. The campground can accommodate RVs up to 27 feet. There is a 14-day stay limit. All sites are available on a first-come, first-served basis; reservations are not accepted. Water is turned off during winter. The campground occasionally fills up on weekends from May through September.

New York

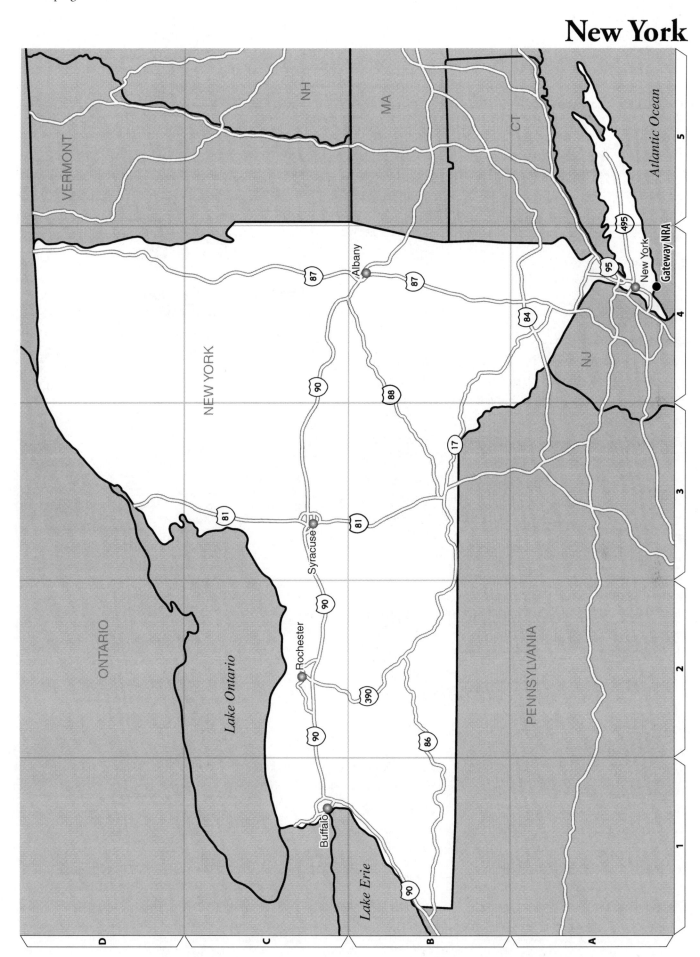

New York Parks

Map	Auto Touring	Biking	Boating	Climbing	Fishing	Hiking	Horseback Riding	Hunting	Snow Skiing	Swimming	Visitor Center	Wildlife Viewing
Gateway National Recreation Area	A4	•	•		•	•	•			•	•	•	•

PARK DETAILS

Gateway National Recreation Area

210 New York Ave
Staten Island, NY 10305
Phone: 718-354-4606

Description

There are three geographic units that make up the 27,000 acres of Gateway National Recreation Area. The units consist of Sandy Hook in New Jersey and Jamaica Bay and Staten Island in New York City. The New York City units include Jamaica Bay Wildlife Refuge, Fort Tilden, Riis Park in Queens, Floyd Bennett Field and Canarsie Pier in Brooklyn. Staten Island has Great Kills Park, Miller Field, and Fort Wadsworth.

Information

Information is available from the Ryan Visitor Center in Floyd Bennett Field. The recently renovated visitor center is open daily year-round (except Christmas and New Year's Day) between 9am and 4:30pm. It features exhibits of the area's history. Information is also available at the Sandy Hook Lighthouse Keepers Quarters Visitor Center, which is open daily from 9am to 5pm. Lighthouse tours are offered between 1pm and 4:30pm.

Fees & Season

The three units of the park are generally open daily year-round from sunrise to sunset. Specific buildings and areas may be open seasonally or on weekends only. There is no entrance fee charged but there is a fee in summer at some areas for beach parking, which varies from $10 to $30 per vehicle, per day.

Directions

Gateway is a vast national park with numerous units scattered across the area. Visitors can arrive at different areas of the park via RV, car, bus, or sometimes by subway or ferry.

RV CAMPING

Floyd Bennett Field Campground

Located about one mile from the park's entrance off Flatbush Ave. Open year-round, 20 sites with picnic tables and grills, $30 per night, drinking water, vault toilets. No pets allowed. There is a 14-day stay limit. Reservations are accepted and can be made online at recreation.gov or by calling 877-444-6777.

North Carolina

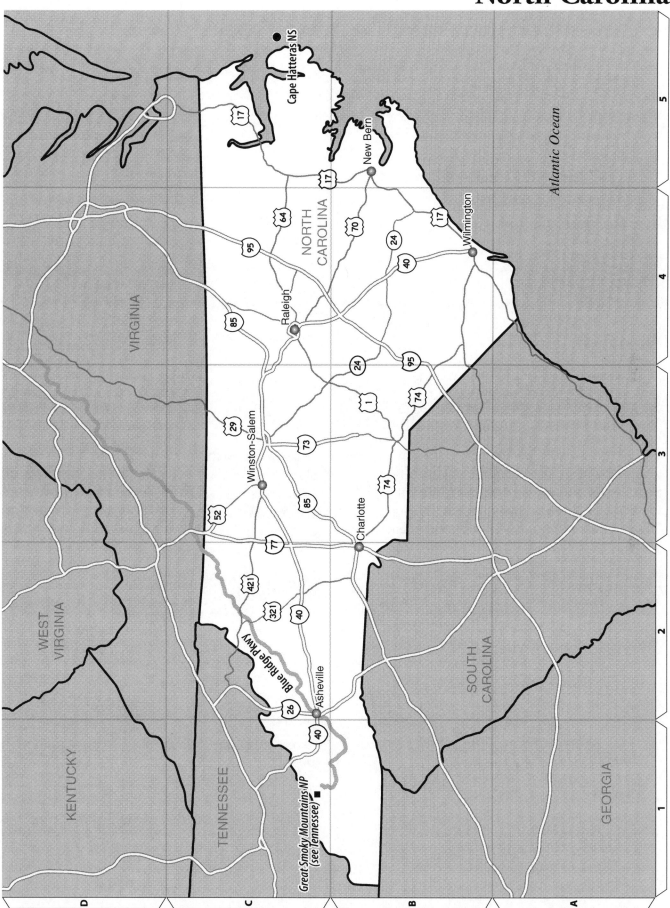

Cape Hatteras NS

Atlantic Ocean

NORTH CAROLINA

New Bern

Wilmington

VIRGINIA

Raleigh

Winston-Salem

Charlotte

Asheville

Blue Ridge Pkwy

Great Smoky Mountains NP
(see Tennessee)

WEST VIRGINIA

KENTUCKY

TENNESSEE

SOUTH CAROLINA

GEORGIA

North Carolina Parks

North Carolina Parks	Map	Auto Touring	Biking	Boating	Climbing	Fishing	Hiking	Horseback Riding	Hunting	Snow Skiing	Swimming	Visitor Center	Wildlife Viewing
Blue Ridge Parkway	C2	•	•	•		•	•	•			•	•	•
Cape Hatteras National Seashore	C5	•	•	•		•	•		•			•	•
Great Smoky Mountains National Park - *see Tennessee*	C1	•	•			•	•	•				•	•

PARK DETAILS

Blue Ridge Parkway

199 Hemphill Knob Rd
Asheville, NC 28803
Phone: 828-348-3400

Description
Blue Ridge Parkway meanders 469 miles between Shenandoah National Park in Virginia and Great Smoky Mountains National Park in North Carolina. The parkway was established in 1936 and encompasses 88,734 acres. It is included in the National Scenic Byways Program as an All-American Road. The parkway is marked every mile by concrete mileposts beginning at MP 0 near Shenandoah National Park and ending at MP 469 at Great Smoky Mountains National Park. Knowing this will help in locating visitor centers and campgrounds.

Information
There are 15 visitor centers along the parkway. Most are generally open from May through October. The Blue Ridge Parkway Visitor Center, Folk Art Center, and the Museum of North Carolina Minerals are open year-round and only close on Thanksgiving, Christmas, and New Year's Day.

Visitor centers are located along the parkway at the following mileposts:

Virginia

Humpback Rocks, Milepost 5.8
James River, Milepost 63.6
Peaks of Otter, Milepost 85.9
Explore Park, Milepost 115

Rocky Knob, Milepost 169.0 (open weekends only)
Blue Ridge Music Center, Milepost 213

North Carolina

Doughton Park, Milepost 241.1
Moses Cone Manor House, Milepost 294.0
Linn Cove, Milepost 304.4
Linville Falls, Milepost 316.4
Museum of North Carolina Minerals, Milepost 331
Craggy Gardens, Milepost 364.5
Folk Art Center, Milepost 382
Blue Ridge Parkway Visitor Center, Milepost 384.5
Waterrock Knob, Milepost 451.2

Fees & Season
Blue Ridge Parkway is typically open all year but weather conditions may cause temporary road closures. The National Park Service maintains a real-time road status map online at https://go.nps.gov/brp-map. There is no fee to travel the route.

Directions
There are entrance and exit points at all major federal and state highways that intersect the route.

RV CAMPING

The following campgrounds are in Virginia.

Otter Creek Campground
Located near milepost 61. Open May through October, 24 RV sites with picnic tables and grills, $20 per night, water, restrooms with flush toilets, dump station, walking trail. Pets welcome. The campground can accommodate large RVs at some sites. Camping is limited to 30 days. Reservations are accepted and can be made online at recreation.gov or by calling 877-444-6777.

Peaks of Otter

Located near milepost 86. Open May through October, 58 RV sites with picnic tables and grills, $20 per night, water, restrooms with flush toilets, dump station, walking trail. Pets welcome. The campground can accommodate large RVs at some sites. Camping is limited to 30 days. Reservations are accepted and can be made online at recreation.gov or by calling 877-444-6777.

Rocky Knob Campground

Located near milepost 167. Open May through October, 28 RV sites with picnic tables and grills, $20 per night, water, restrooms with flush toilets, dump station, walking trail. Pets welcome. The campground can accommodate large RVs at some sites. Camping is limited to 30 days. Reservations are accepted and can be made online at recreation.gov or by calling 877-444-6777.

The following campgrounds are in North Carolina.

Doughton Park Campground

Located near milepost 241. Open May through October, 25 RV sites with picnic tables and grills, $20 per night, water, restrooms with flush toilets, dump station, walking trail. Pets welcome. The campground can accommodate large RVs at some sites. Camping is limited to 30 days. Reservations are accepted and can be made online at recreation.gov or by calling 877-444-6777.

Julian Price Campground

Located near milepost 297. Open May through October, 78 RV sites with picnic tables and grills, $20 per night, water, restrooms with flush toilets, showers, dump station, walking trail. Pets welcome. The campground can accommodate large RVs at some sites. Camping is limited to 30 days. Reservations are accepted and can be made online at recreation.gov or by calling 877-444-6777.

Linville Falls Campground

Located near milepost 316. Open May through October, 20 RV sites with picnic tables and grills, $20 per night, water, restrooms with flush toilets, dump station, walking trail. Pets welcome. The campground can accommodate large RVs at some sites. Camping is limited to 30 days. Reservations are accepted and can be made online at recreation.gov or by calling 877-444-6777.

Crabtree Falls Campground

Located near milepost 339.5. Open May through October, 22 RV sites with picnic tables and grills, $20 per night, water, restrooms with flush toilets, dump station, walking trail. Pets welcome. The campground can accommodate large RVs at some sites. Camping is limited to 30 days. Sites are available on a first-come, first-served basis; reservations are not accepted.

Mount Pisgah Campground

Located near milepost 408. Open May through October, 62 RV sites with picnic tables and grills, $20 per night, water, restrooms with flush toilets, showers, dump station, walking trail. Pets welcome. The campground can accommodate large RVs at some sites. Camping is limited to 30 days. Reservations are accepted and can be made online at recreation.gov or by calling 877-444-6777.

PARK DETAILS

Cape Hatteras National Seashore

1401 National Park Dr
Manteo, NC 27954
Phone: 252-473-2111

Description

Cape Hatteras National Seashore was established in 1953 and protects over 30,000 acres of three barrier islands: Bodie Island, Hatteras Island, Ocracoke Island. Beach and sound access ramps, nature trails, and lighthouses can be found on all three islands. From April to mid-October, the Cape Hatteras Lighthouse and the Bodie Island Lighthouse are open for climbing. Nearly 2.5 million people come to the park each year.

Information

Information is available from three visitor centers. Bodie Island Visitor Center is about seven miles south of Whalebone Junction off SR-12. Hatteras Island Visitor Center is near Buxton off SR-12 in the Cape Hatteras Lighthouse. Ocracoke Visitor Center is off NC 12 in Ocracoke. All of the visitor centers remain open year-round except on Christmas Day.

Fees & Season

The park generally remains open all year. No entrance fee is charged. Fees are charged for the self-guided lighthouse climbs, off-road vehicle use, and camping.

Directions

Cape Hatteras National Seashore is in eastern North Carolina. The northern entrance is located at the junction of US-64 and SR-12 near Nags Head. The southern entrance is located on SR-12 near Ocracoke Village, which is accessible by ferry only.

RV CAMPING

Cape Point Campground

Located two miles south of Buxton off SR-12 near the Cape Hatteras Lighthouse. Open April through November, 202 sites with picnic tables and grills, $20 per night, drinking water, restrooms with flush toilets, cold showers, dump station nearby. Pets welcome. The campground can accommodate large RVs at some sites. There is a 14-day stay limit. Reservations are accepted and can be made online at recreation.gov or by calling 877-444-6777.

Frisco Campground

Located east of Frisco off SR-12. Open late April through November, 127 sites with picnic tables and grills, $28 per night, drinking water, restrooms with flush toilets, cold showers. Pets welcome. The campground can accommodate large RVs at some sites. There is a 14-day stay limit. Reservations are accepted and can be made online at recreation.gov or by calling 877-444-6777.

Ocracoke Campground

Located off SR-12 about four miles east of Ocracoke, which is only accessible by ferry. Open April through November, 136 sites with picnic tables and grills, $28 per night, drinking water, restrooms with flush toilets, cold showers, dump station. Pets welcome. The campground can accommodate large RVs at some sites. There is a 14-day stay limit. Reservations are accepted and can be made online at recreation.gov or by calling 877-444-6777.

Oregon Inlet Campground

Located off SR-12 about 12 miles south of Nags Head. Open April through November, 120 sites with picnic tables and grills, $28 per night, 27 sites have utility hookups for $35 per night, drinking water, restrooms with flush toilets, cold showers, dump station nearby. Pets welcome. The campground can accommodate large RVs at some sites. There is a 14-day stay limit. Reservations are accepted and can be made online at recreation.gov or by calling 877-444-6777.

North Dakota

North Dakota Parks

	Map	Auto Touring	Biking	Boating	Climbing	Fishing	Hiking	Horseback Riding	Hunting	Snow Skiing	Swimming	Visitor Center	Wildlife Viewing
Theodore Roosevelt National Park	B1	•	•	•		•	•	•				•	•

PARK DETAILS

Theodore Roosevelt National Park

PO Box 7
Medora, ND 58645
Phone: 701-623-4466

Description

Established in 1947, the 70,447-acre park protects badlands along the Little Missouri River and part of Theodore Roosevelt's Elkhorn Ranch. The park is divided into three units; the North Unit, the South Unit, and the Elkhorn Ranch Unit. Park roads in the North and South Units provide numerous overlooks for viewing the surrounding landscape. Numerous trails are also within each unit for the more adventurous explorer. The Elkhorn Ranch Unit protects the location of Roosevelt's "home ranch" in the Badlands. The only tangible remains of the ranch are the foundation stones of the buildings.

Information

Information is available from three visitor centers. Medora Visitor Center is located near Medora at the entrance to the South Unit off I-94. It is open daily all year from 8am to 4:30pm; summer hours are 8am to 5pm. It closes on Thanksgiving, Christmas, and New Year's Day. A museum features Theodore Roosevelt collections, exhibits on history, nature, and geology.

The North Unit Visitor Center is just west of US-85 about 50 miles north of Belfield at I-94 Exit 42. A temporary visitor center has been opened near the North Unit entrance and is open daily from 9am to 5pm. The original building was demolished due to a structural failure. Planning for a new facility is underway.

Painted Canyon Visitor Center is off I-94 at Exit 32 in the South Unit. It is generally open May through October from 8:30am to 4:30pm. This visitor center offers panoramic views, wildlife viewing, hiking trails, and a picnic area.

Fees & Season

The park is open all year but roads within the park may temporarily close in winter due to snow and ice. Also, the North Unit operates on Central Time, while the South Unit operates on Mountain Time. An entrance fee of $30 per vehicle is charged and is valid for seven days.

Directions

Theodore Roosevelt National Park is in southwest North Dakota about 135 miles west of Bismarck. The South Unit is accessed from I-94 at Exit 24 or Exit 27 (westbound exit only). The North Unit is approximately 50 miles north of I-94 Exit 42 via US-85. The Elkhorn Ranch Unit is accessible via a 35-mile drive over gravel roads; conditions can vary and a high-clearance vehicle is recommended.

RV CAMPING

Cottonwood Campground

Located six miles from the South Unit park entrance. Open all year, 64 sites with picnic tables and grills, $14 per night, drinking water, restrooms with flush toilets. The campground has some pull-through sites. In winter, rates are reduced and amenities are limited. Pets welcome. There is a 14-day stay limit. Reservations are accepted and can be made online at recreation.gov or by calling 877-444-6777.

Juniper Campground

Located four miles from the North Unit park entrance. Open all year, 50 sites with picnic tables and grills, $14 per night, drinking water, restrooms with flush toilets, dump station. The campground has some pull-through sites. In winter, rates are reduced and amenities are limited. Pets welcome. There is a 14-day stay limit. All sites are available on a first-come, first-served basis; reservations are not accepted.

Oklahoma

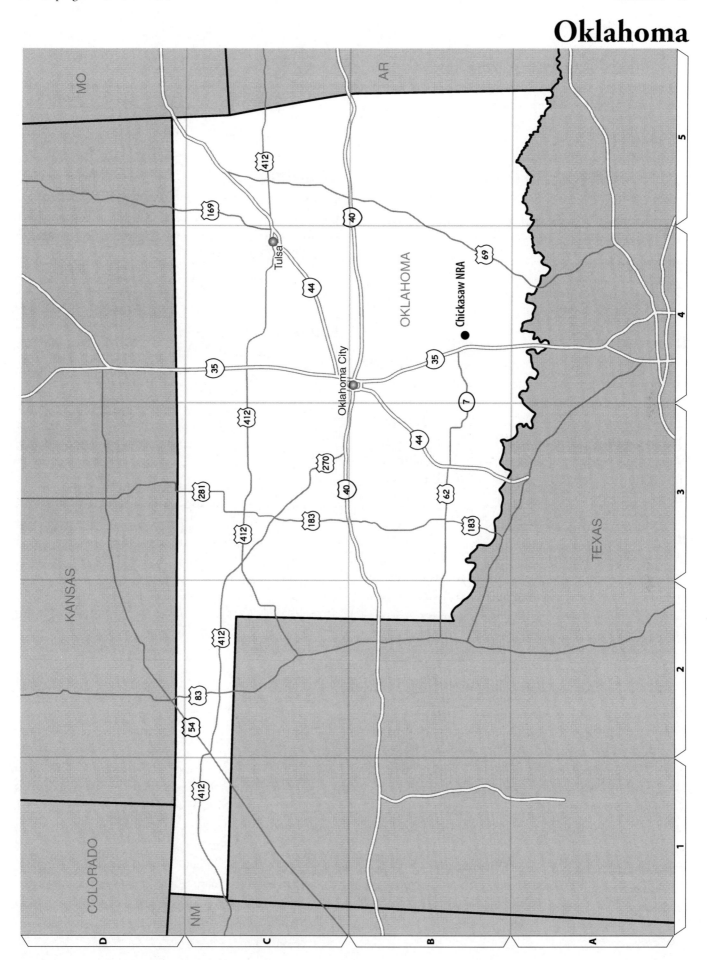

Oklahoma Parks

	Map	Auto Touring	Biking	Boating	Climbing	Fishing	Hiking	Horseback Riding	Hunting	Snow Skiing	Swimming	Visitor Center	Wildlife Viewing
Chickasaw National Recreation Area	B4	•	•	•		•	•	•	•		•	•	•

PARK DETAILS

Chickasaw National Recreation Area

901 W First St
Sulphur, OK 73086
Phone: 580-622-7234

Description

Chickasaw National Recreation Area was originally established as Sulphur Springs Reservation in 1902; it was later renamed and redesignated in 1976. The park encompasses nearly 10,000 acres of springs, streams, and lakes. The park receives about 1.5 million visitors each year. Most park visitors come for the boating and fishing but the park also offers over 20 miles of hiking trails and horseback riding.

Information

Information is available from the Chickasaw Visitor Center in Sulphur at the corner of Broadway Avenue and US-177. The visitor center is open daily all year from 9am to 6pm; it closes on Thanksgiving and Christmas Day. It features an information desk, multi-purpose gallery, gift shop, media room, and complimentary coffee.

Information is also available from the Travertine Nature Center, located on Travertine Creek near the eastern edge of the Platt Historic District. The nature center is open all year except on Thanksgiving Day, Christmas Day, and New Year's Day. Daily activities are scheduled throughout the summer including nature walks and campfire programs.

Fees & Season

The recreation area is open year-round. No entrance fee is charged.

Directions

Chickasaw National Recreation Area is in south-central Oklahoma about 80 miles south of Oklahoma City. Portions of the recreation area are accessible primarily from US-177 and SR-7.

RV CAMPING

Buckhorn Campground

Located nine miles south of Sulphur via US-177 and Buckhorn Road. There are four loops within the campground as described below. An RV dump station is located outside of the campground about .7 mile west along Buckhorn Road.

Loop A: Open mid-May to mid-September, 16 RV sites with picnic tables and fire rings, $16 per night, drinking water, restrooms with flush toilets, showers. There is a 14-day stay limit. The campground can accommodate large RVs at some sites. All sites are available on a first-come, first-served basis; reservations are not accepted.

Loop B: Open mid-May to mid-September, 5 RV sites with picnic tables and fire rings, $16 per night, drinking water, restrooms with flush toilets, showers. There is a 14-day stay limit. The campground can accommodate large RVs at some sites. All sites are available on a first-come, first-served basis; reservations are not accepted.

Loop C: Open March through November, 28 RV sites with picnic tables and fire rings, $16 per night, 24 sites have water and electric hookups for $22 to $24 per night, drinking water, restrooms with flush toilets, showers. Pets welcome. There is a 14-day stay limit. The campground can accommodate large RVs at some sites. Reservations are accepted and can be made online at recreation.gov or by calling 877-444-6777.

Loop D: Open year-round, 37 RV sites with picnic tables and fire rings, $16 per night, 24 sites have water and electric hookups for $22 to $24 per night, drinking water, restrooms with flush toilets, showers. Pets welcome. There is a 14-day stay limit. The campground can accommodate large RVs at some sites. All sites are available on a first-come, first-served basis; reservations are not accepted.

The Point Campground

Located about seven miles southwest of Sulphur via SR-7 and Charles F. Cooper Memorial Rd. There are two loops within the campground as described below. An RV dump station is located along the campground entrance road.

Lower Loop: Open all year, nine RV sites with picnic tables and fire rings, all sites have water and electric hookups, $22 per night, drinking water, restrooms with flush toilets, showers. Pets welcome. There is a 14-day stay limit. The campground can accommodate large RVs at some sites. Sites are available on a first-come, first-served basis; reservations not accepted.

Upper Loop: Open all year, 12 RV sites with picnic tables and fire rings, all sites have water and electric hookups, $22 per night, drinking water, restrooms with flush toilets, showers. Pets welcome. There is a 14-day stay limit. The campground can accommodate large RVs at some sites. Reservations are accepted and can be made online at recreation.gov or by calling 877-444-6777.

Oregon

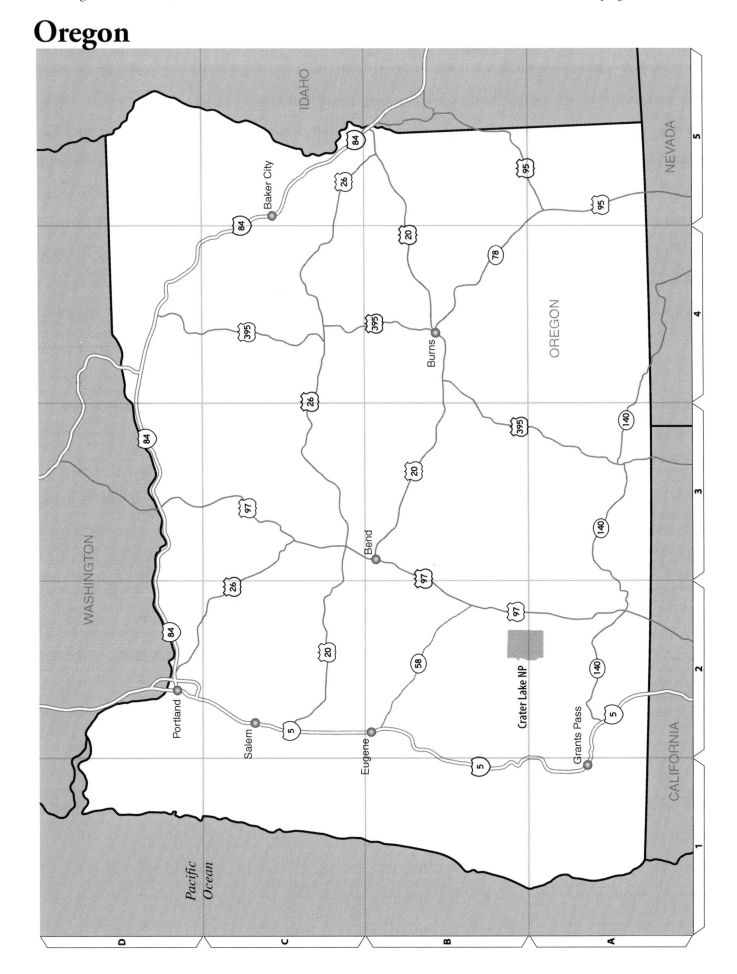

Oregon Parks

Crater Lake National Park	Map	Auto Touring	Biking	Boating	Climbing	Fishing	Hiking	Horseback Riding	Hunting	Snow Skiing	Swimming	Visitor Center	Wildlife Viewing
Crater Lake National Park	B2	•	•			•	•					•	•

PARK DETAILS

Crater Lake National Park

PO Box 7
Crater Lake, OR 97604
Phone: 541-594-3000

Description

Crater Lake is the deepest in the United States and is widely known for its intense blue color. The park was established in 1902 and encompasses 183,244 acres. Those interested in hiking will find numerous trails ranging from easy to strenuous. Part of the Pacific Crest National Scenic Trail also crosses the park. The park receives more than 700,000 visitors annually.

Information

Information is available from two visitor centers. Rim Visitor Center is open daily from late May to September. A gift shop, cafeteria, and Crater Lake Lodge are nearby. Visitor center hours are 9:30am to 5pm daily. Steel Visitor Center is inside the park headquarters along Rim Drive. It remains open all year and is open daily 9am to 5pm from late April to early November and 10am to 4pm daily from early November to early April. A short film and exhibits of the park and its history are available.

Fees & Season

The park is generally open all year but some of the roads and facilities close during winter. An entrance fee of $25 per vehicle is charged and is valid for seven days.

Directions

Crater Lake National Park is in southwest Oregon about 75 miles north of Klamath Falls via US-97 and SR-62.

RV CAMPING

Mazama Campground

Concessionaire campground located just off SR-62 in Mazama Villiage. Open mid-June to late September weather permitting, 214 sites with picnic tables and fire rings, $32.50 per night, drinking water, restrooms with flush toilets, dump station, coin-operated showers, laundry facilities, camper store, gas station. Pets welcome. The campground can accommodate RVs up to 50 feet. There is a 14-day stay limit. Reservations are accepted and can be made online at craterlakelodges. com or by calling 888-774-2728.

Pennsylvania

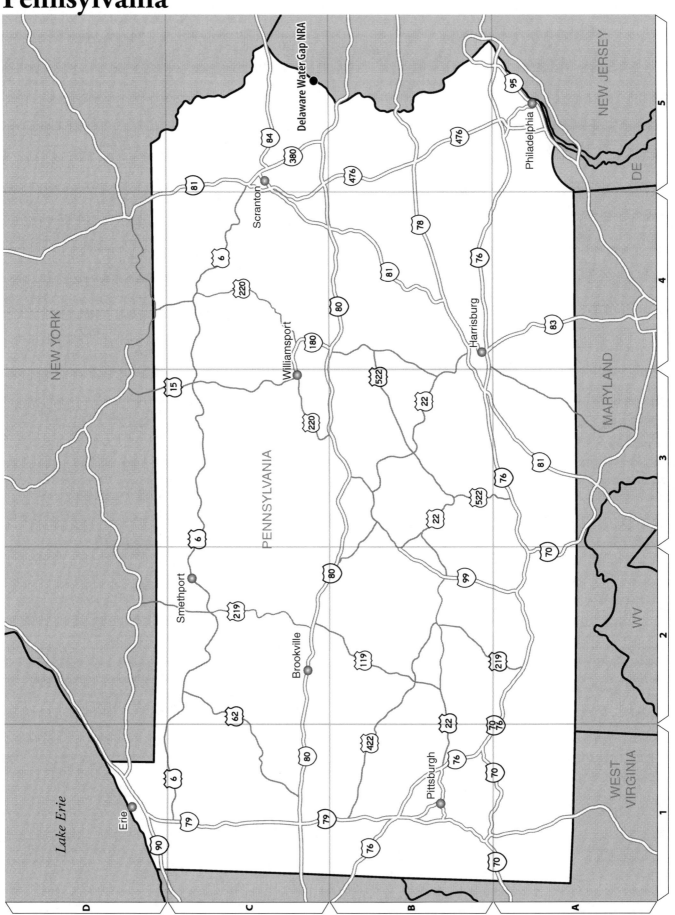

Pennsylvania Parks

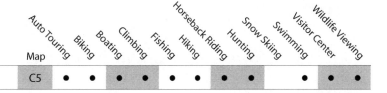

Delaware Water Gap National Recreation Area	Map	Auto Touring	Biking	Boating	Climbing	Fishing	Hiking	Horseback Riding	Hunting	Snow Skiing	Swimming	Visitor Center	Wildlife Viewing
	C5	•	•	•	•	•	•	•	•		•	•	•

PARK DETAILS

Delaware Water Gap National Recreation Area

1978 River Road
Bushkill, PA 18324
Phone: 570-426-2452

Description

Delaware Water Gap National Recreation Area preserves 40 miles of the Middle Delaware River and nearly 70,000 acres of land along the river's shore in New Jersey and Pennsylvania. It was established in 1965. In 1978, the river was designated a National Scenic River. Around five million visitors come to the park each year to float the river, fish the numerous streams, or walk part of the Appalachian Trail, among other things.

Information

Information is available from two visitor centers. Dinghmans Falls Visitor Center is open mid-May to late Spring; hours vary. The visitor center is west of US-209 at SR-739 and has exhibits, a book store, and guided walks to Dingmans and Silverthread waterfalls. Kittatinny Point Visitor Center is open on weekends in summer from 9am to 5pm. The visitor center is located in New Jersey off I-80 and has exhibits, a book store, and access to the Appalachian National Scenic Trail. Information is also available from the park's headquarters along River Road in Bushkill, Pennsylvania. The office is open weekdays year-round from 8:30am to 4:30pm; it closes on federal holidays. It is open daily in summer.

Fees & Season

The park remains open year-round but some roads close in winter. No entrance fee is charged but some areas charge an amenity fee.

Directions

Delaware Water Gap National Recreation Area is in northeast Pennsylvania about 50 miles east of Scranton. The park lies between I-84 to the north and I-80 in the south, both providing access to the park via US-209 and US-206.

RV CAMPING

Dingmans Campground

Concessionaire campground located along US-209 in Dingmans Ferry, Pennsylvania. Open April through October, 50 RV sites with picnic tables and fire rings, $42 to $44 per night, water and electric hookups available at some sites, potable water, restrooms with flush toilets, showers, dump station, camp store. There is a 14-day stay limit. Reservations are accepted and can be made by calling 570-828-1551 or 877-828-1551.

South Dakota

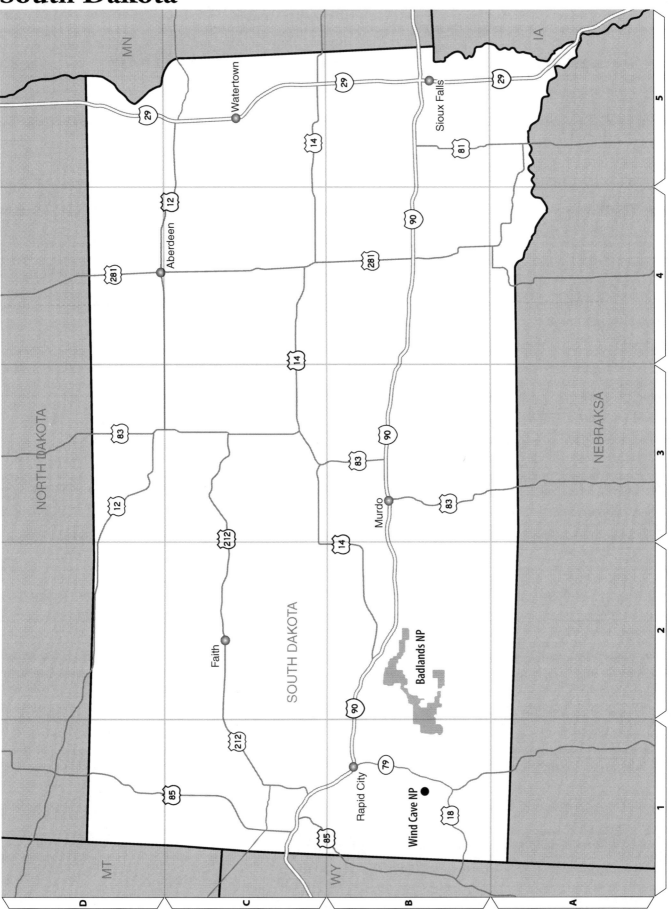

South Dakota Parks

	Map	Auto Touring	Biking	Boating	Climbing	Fishing	Hiking	Horseback Riding	Hunting	Snow Skiing	Swimming	Visitor Center	Wildlife Viewing
Badlands National Park	B2	•	•	•			•	•				•	•
Wind Cave National Park	B1	•	•				•	•				•	•

PARK DETAILS

Badlands National Park

25216 Ben Reifel Rd
Interior, SD 57750
Phone: 605-433-5361

Description

Badlands National Park was established in 1929. It consists of 244,000 acres of sharply eroded buttes, pinnacles, and spires surrounded by the largest, protected mixed-grass prairie in the United States. The park features one of the most complete fossil accumulations in North America. Approximately one million people come to the park annually; visitation is highest during summer.

Information

Information is available from the Ben Reifel Visitor Center on SR-240 about 8 miles south of I-90 Exit 131. The visitor center is open daily all year and features exhibits of fossils, cultural history, and prairie ecology. Summer hours are 7am to 7pm. It closes on Thanksgiving, Christmas, and New Year's Day. Information is also available at the White River Visitor Center on Highway 27 in the Pine Ridge Indian Reservation. It is open daily in summer between 9am and 5pm.

Fees & Season

The park remains open year-round. An entrance fee of $25 is charged and is valid for seven days.

Directions

Badlands National Park is in southwest South Dakota about 80 miles southeast of Rapid City. The park lies to the south of Interstate 90 and can be accessed from exit 110 and 131. The park is also accessible from points along SR-44.

RV CAMPING

Cedar Pass Campground

Concessionaire managed campground about 8.5 miles south of I-90 Exit 131. Open April through October, 30 RV sites with shaded picnic tables, $37 per night sites with electric hookups, restrooms with flush toilets, dump station, showers and water nearby. Campfires and charcoal fires are not permitted. There is a 14-day stay limit. Reservations are accepted and can be made online at cedarpasslodge.com or by calling 877-386-4383.

PARK DETAILS

Wind Cave National Park

26611 US Highway 385
Hot Springs, SD 57747
Phone: 605-745-4600

Description

Wind Cave National Park was established in 1903. It features one of the world's longest and most complex caves beneath 28,295 acres of mixed-grass prairie and ponderosa pine forest. Various ranger-guided tours are offered for exploring the different parts of the cave. Tickets are sold on a first-come, first-served basis; long waits may be encountered during peak summer visitation. Reservations are available for some tours.

Information

Information is available from the Wind Cave Visitor Center located 11 miles north of Hot Springs via US-385. The center is open all year except on Thanksgiving, Christmas, and New Year's Day. Hours are typically 8am to 7pm in summer and 8am to 4:30 in winter. All cave tours depart from the visitor center. Exhibits feature cave exploration, formations, and history.

Fees & Season

The park is generally open year-round but snow can limit access to some remote areas in winter. There is no entrance fee but fees are collected for cave tours and vary from $10 to $30.

Directions

Wind Cave National Park is in southwest South Dakota about 50 miles south of Rapid City. The park is accessible from US-385 and SR-87.

RV CAMPING

Elk Mountain Campground

Located northwest of the park's visitor center off US-385. Open all year, 75 sites with picnic tables and fire rings, $18 per night, drinking water, restrooms with flush toilets, pit toilets in winter. From late fall to early spring when the water is turned off, the camping fee is half. Pets welcome. There is a 14-day stay limit. Sites are available on a first-come, first-served basis; reservations are not accepted. The campground rarely fills.

Tennessee

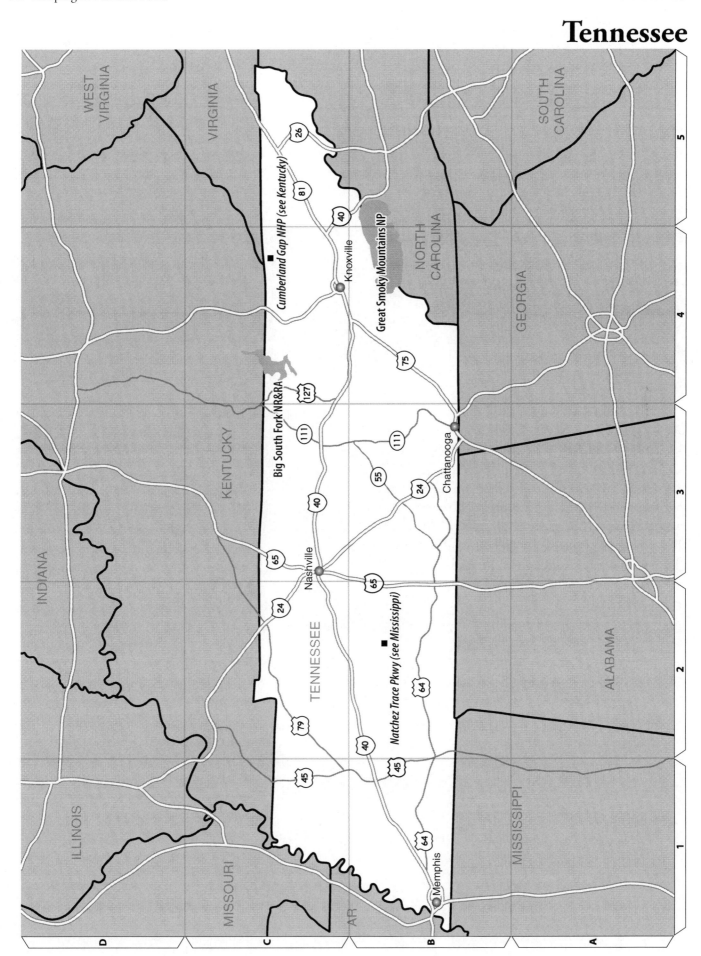

Tennessee Parks

	Map	Auto Touring	Biking	Boating	Climbing	Fishing	Hiking	Horseback Riding	Hunting	Snow Skiing	Swimming	Visitor Center	Wildlife Viewing
Big South Fork National River and Recreation Area	C4		•	•	•	•	•	•	•		•	•	•
Cumberland Gap National Historical Park - *see Kentucky*	C4	•	•				•		•		•	•	•
Great Smoky Mountains National Park	B4	•	•			•	•	•				•	•
Natchez Trace Parkway - *see Mississippi*	B2	•	•	•		•	•	•				•	•

PARK DETAILS

Big South Fork National River and Recreation Area

4564 Leatherwood Rd
Oneida, TN 37841
Phone: 423-569-9778

Description

Big South Fork National River and Recreation Area was established in 1974 and encompasses 125,242 acres. It protects 90 miles of the Big South Fork of the Cumberland River and its tributaries. Around 600,000 visitors come to the park to enjoy fishing or floating the river. The park also features over 400 miles of trails for hiking, horseback riding, or mountain biking.

Information

Information is available from one visitor center located within the park. Bandy Creek Visitor Center is about 15 miles west of Oneida, Tennessee, off SR-297. It is open year-round except on Christmas Day; hours are 8am to 6pm from Memorial Day to Labor Day and 9am to 5pm the rest of the year. Information is also available weekdays from the park's headquarters along SR-297 about three miles past the park entrance; hours are 8am to 4:30pm.

Fees & Season

The park is open year-round but some facilities close during the winter. No entrance fee is charged.

Directions

Big South Fork National River and Recreation Area is in northeast Tennessee and southern Kentucky. The park lies west of US-27 and can be accessed from various highways but primarily SR-297, west of Oneida, Tennessee.

RV CAMPING

Bandy Creek Campground

Located off SR-297 about 15 miles west of Oneida, Tennessee. Open year-round, 93 RV sites with water and 30-amp electric ($25 per night), 5 RV sites with water and 50-amp service ($32 per night), picnic tables, fire rings, drinking water, restrooms with flush toilets, showers, dump station. Additional amenities include a swimming pool, volleyball court, playground areas, and game fields. Pets welcome. The campground can accommodate large RVs at most sites. There is a 14-day stay limit. Reservations are accepted and can be made online at recreation.gov or by calling 877-444-6777.

Blue Heron Campground

Located off SR-742 about nine miles west of Stearns, Kentucky. Open April through November, 45 sites with water and electric hookups, $20 per night, picnic tables, fire rings, drinking water, restrooms with flush toilets, showers, dump station. Pets welcome. The campground can accommodate large RVs at most sites. There is a 14-day stay limit. Reservations are accepted and can be made online at recreation.gov or by calling 877-444-6777.

PARK DETAILS

Great Smoky Mountains National Park

107 Park Headquarters Rd
Gatlinburg, TN 37738
Phone: 865-436-1200

Description

Around ten million people come to the Great Smoky Mountains National Park each year, making it the most visited national park. Established in 1934, the park protects more than 521,000 acres of the Southern Appalachians. Newfound Gap Road (US-441) is a heavily used 33-mile route across the park, connecting Gatlinburg, Tennessee, with Cherokee, North Carolina. The route has numerous pullouts for viewing the surrounding mountains. The route provides access to the park's highest point, 6,643-foot Clingmans Dome where an overlook provides spectacular views into the park.

Information

Information is available from the following four visitor centers within the park:

Sugarlands Visitor Center is about two miles south of Gatlinburg, Tennessee, on US-441. It is open year-round except Christmas Day. In summer, the visitor center is open daily from 8am to 7pm. Hours are shortened the rest of the year. A 20-minute film about the park is shown here.

Cades Cove Visitor Center is about 30 miles west of Gatlinburg, Tennessee. It is near the midpoint of the 11-mile, one-way, Cades Cove Loop Road. It is open year-round except Christmas Day. Summer hours are 9am to 7pm; hours are shortened the rest of the year. Features include indoor and outdoor exhibits of southern Appalachian Mountain life including a grist mill and other historic structures.

Oconaluftee Visitor Center is about two miles north of Cherokee, North Carolina, on US-441. It is open all year except Christmas Day. Summer hours are 8am to 7pm; hours are shortened the rest of the year. Adjacent to the visitor center is the Mountain Farm Museum and Mingus Mill, which features a collection of historic log buildings gathered from throughout the region and preserved on a single site.

Clingmans Dome Visitor Contact Station is seven miles off US-441 near the Tennessee and North Carolina state line. The visitor center is open April through November. In summer, the visitor contact station is open from 10am to 6:30pm. Hours are shortened in spring and fall. An observation tower here provides some really nice views of the surrounding mountains.

Fees & Season

The park remains open year-round but some secondary roads and visitor facilities may close in winter. No entrance fee is charged.

Directions

Great Smoky Mountains National Park is in eastern Tennessee and western North Carolina. It is accessible from points along Interstate 40 and various other highways, primarily US-441.

RV CAMPING

Abrams Creek Campground

Located about seven miles north of Chilhowee, Tennessee, off US-129. Open late April to mid-October, 16 sites with picnic tables and fire grates, $17.50 per night, drinking water, restrooms with flush toilets. Pets welcome. The campground can only accommodate small RVs up to 12 feet. There is a 14-day stay limit. Reservations are required and can be made online at recreation.gov or by calling 877-444-6777.

Balsam Mountain Campground

Located 23 miles northeast of Cherokee, North Carolina, via US-19, Blue Ridge Parkway, and Heintooga Ridge Rd. Open mid-May to mid-October, 46 sites with picnic tables and fire grates, $17.50 per night, drinking water, restrooms with flush toilets. Pets welcome. The campground can accommodate RVs up to 24 feet. There is a 14-day stay limit. Reservations are required and can be made online at recreation.gov or by calling 877-444-6777. Only RVs with slide outs on one side can be accommodated due to parallel parking and the narrow campground road.

Cades Cove Campground

Located 11 miles southwest of Townsend, Tennessee, via SR-73 and Laurel Creek Rd. Open year-round, 130 sites with picnic tables and fire grates, $25 per night, drinking water, restrooms with flush toilets, camp store, dump station. Pets welcome. The campground can accommodate trailers up to 35 feet and motor homes up to 40 feet. There is a 14-day stay limit. Reservations are accepted and can be made online at recreation.gov or by calling 877-444-6777.

Cataloochee Campground

Located in North Carolina about 11 miles west of Interstate 40 Exit 20 via US-276 and Cove Creek Road. Open March through October, 27 sites with picnic tables and fire grates, $25 per night, drinking water, restrooms with flush toilets. Pets welcome. The campground can accommodate trailers up to 25 feet and motor homes up to 31 feet. There is a 14-day stay limit. Reservations are required and can be made online at recreation.gov or by calling 877-444-6777. Access to the campground is via a narrow, winding, mountain road with some steep drop-offs and no guard rails. A three-mile stretch of gravel road contains many narrow, blind curves. It may be necessary to stop or back up to allow other vehicles to pass. Use extreme caution while traveling this route.

Cosby Campground

Located about three miles south of Cosby, Tennessee, via US-321 and SR-32. Open April through October, 19 RV sites with picnic tables and fire grates, $17.50 per night, drinking water, restrooms with flush toilets, dump station. Pets welcome. The campground can accommodate RVs up to 25 feet. There is a 14-day stay limit. Reservations are accepted and can be made online at recreation.gov or by calling 877-444-6777.

Deep Creek Campground

Located about 2.5 miles north of Bryson City, North Carolina, via Deep Creek Road. Open April through October, 50 RV sites with picnic tables and fire grates, $21 per night, drinking water, restrooms with flush toilets, dump station. Pets welcome. The campground can accommodate RVs up to 26 feet. There is a 14-day stay limit. Sites are available on a first-come, first-served basis; reservations are not accepted.

Elkmont Campground

Located eight miles southwest of Gatlinburg, Tennessee, via US 441 and Fighting Creek Gap Road. Open mid-March to late November, 147 RV sites with picnic tables and fire grates, $25 to $27 per night, drinking water, restrooms with flush toilets. Pets welcome. The campground can accommodate trailers up to 32 feet and motor homes up to 35 feet. There is a 14-day stay limit. Reservations are accepted and can be made online at recreation.gov or by calling 877-444-6777.

Smokemont Campground

Located about seven miles north of Cherokee, North Carolina, via US-441. Open year-round, 68 RV sites with picnic tables and fire grates, $25 per night, drinking water, restrooms with flush toilets, dump station. Pets welcome. The campground can accommodate trailers up to 35 feet and motor homes up to 40 feet. There is a 14-day stay limit. Reservations are accepted and can be made online at recreation.gov or by calling 877-444-6777.

Texas

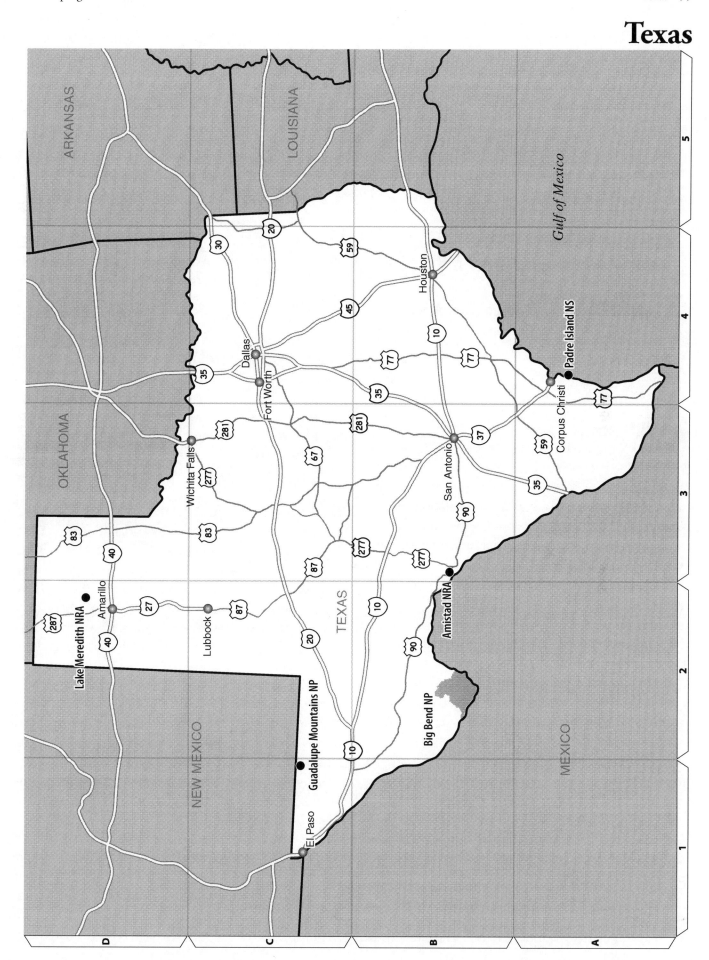

Texas Parks

	Map	Auto Touring	Biking	Boating	Climbing	Fishing	Hiking	Horseback Riding	Hunting	Snow Skiing	Swimming	Visitor Center	Wildlife Viewing
Amistad National Recreation Area	B3			•		•	•		•		•	•	•
Big Bend National Park	B2			•		•	•					•	•
Guadalupe Mountains National Park	C1					•	•					•	•
Lake Meredith National Recreation Area	D2			•		•	•		•	•		•	•
Padre Island National Seashore	A4	•	•	•		•	•		•			•	•

PARK DETAILS

Amistad National Recreation Area

4121 Veterans Blvd
Del Rio, TX 78840
Phone: 830-775-7491

Description

Amistand National Recreation Area consists of the U.S. portion of the International Amistad Reservoir. The recreation area was established in 1990 and protects over 57,000 acres. More than one million people come to the park each year to enjoy boating, fishing, camping, hiking, rock art viewing and the area's rich cultural history.

Information

Information is available from the Amistad Visitor Information Center on US-90, northwest of Del Rio. The center is open daily from 8am to 4:30pm all year except Christmas Day. Exhibits relate the story of the dam's construction and describe the natural and cultural resources surrounding the reservoir. Several movies can be viewed in the theater. The Big Bend Natural History Association operates a book store inside the visitor center.

Fees & Season

The recreation area remains open all year. No entrance fee is charged but activity fees are charged for boating, hunting, and camping.

Directions

Amistad National Recreation Area is in southwest Texas about 150 miles west of San Antonio via US-90. Access to the park from the north is via US-277/US-377.

RV CAMPING

277 North Campground

Located about 10 miles north of Del Rio off US-277. Open year-round, 17 sites with picnic tables and fire grates, $4 per night, vault toilets. Pets welcome. There is a 14-day stay limit. Sites are available on a first-come, first-served basis; reservations are not accepted. The campground rarely fills except on holiday weekends.

Governors Landing

Located about 12 miles west of Del Rio off US-90. Open year-round, 15 sites with picnic tables and fire grates, $8 per night, vault toilets. Pets welcome. The campground can accommodate RVs up to 28 feet. There is a 14-day stay limit. Sites are available on a first-come, first-served basis; reservations are not accepted. The campground rarely fills except on holiday weekends.

Rough Canyon

Located 14 miles north of Del Rio and seven miles west of US-277. Open year-round, four sites with picnic tables and fire grates, $4 per night, vault toilets. Pets welcome. There is a 14-day stay limit. Sites are available on a first-come, first-served basis; reservations are not accepted. The campground rarely fills except on holiday weekends.

San Pedro Campground

Located seven miles west of Del Rio off US-90. Open year-round, 30 sites with picnic tables and fire grates, $4 per night, vault toilets. Pets welcome. There is a 14-day stay limit. Sites are available on a first-come, first-served basis; reservations are not accepted. The campground rarely fills except on holiday weekends.

Spur 406 Campground

Located about 28 miles northwest of Del Rio via US-90 and SR-406. Open year-round, six sites with picnic tables and fire grates, $4 per night, vault toilets. Pets welcome. There is a 14-day stay limit. Sites are available on a first-come, first-served basis; reservations are not accepted. The campground rarely fills except on holiday weekends.

PARK DETAILS

Big Bend National Park

PO Box 129
Big Bend National Park, TX 79834
Phone: 432-477-2251

Description

Big Bend National Park was established in 1944 and is one of the largest and least visited national parks in America. The park protects more than 800,000 acres of desert landscape, mountains, and deep canyons carved by the Rio Grande River.

Scenic Drives

Ross Maxwell Scenic Drive is a 30-mile route that leads to the Castolon Historic District and Santa Elena Canyon. The Castolon Historic District was established as a cavalry camp in the early Twentieth Century. A visitor center, campground, and store now reside in the area. At the end of the scenic drive is a trail that follows the Rio Grande River upstream into Santa Elena Canyon. Several overlooks along the route provide not only scenic views of the surrounding landscape but access to hiking trails and historic landmarks.

Information

Information is available from the following visitor centers within the park:

Castolon Visitor Center is located in the southwest part of the park near the Cottonwood Campground about 35 miles southwest of park headquarters. It is open seasonally from November through April; hours are 10am to 4pm. It closes during the lunch hour.

Chisos Basin Visitor Center is open all year from 8:30am to 4pm; it closes during the lunch hour. The visitor center is about nine miles southwest of the park headquarters. The road is not recommended for RVs over 24 feet because of sharp curves and steep grades.

Panther Junction Visitor Center is 26 miles from the north entrance and is located near the park headquarters. It remains open all year; hours are 9am to 5pm. It is probably the best place to begin your visit. Backcountry and river use permits are issued during normal business hours and entrance fees can be paid here. Interactive exhibits provide an overview of the natural and cultural history of the park. A park orientation movie is presented in the theater every 30 minutes.

Persimmon Gap Visitor Center is located along the main park road near the park's northern entrance off US-385. It is open seasonally from November through April; hours are 9:30am to 4pm. It closes during the lunch hour. The visitor center has exhibits, bookstore, mini-theater, and restrooms. Entrance fees can be paid here.

Rio Grande Village Visitor Center is located in the eastern part of the park about 20 miles southeast of park headquarters. It is open seasonally from November through April; hours are 8:30am to 4pm. It closes during the lunch hour.

Fees & Season

The park is open year-round. An entrance fee of $30 per vehicle is charged and is valid for seven days.

Directions

Big Bend National Park is in west Texas about 98 miles south of I-10 in Fort Stockton via US-385.

RV CAMPING

Chisos Basin Campground

Located about nine miles southwest of the park headquarters. Open all year, 60 sites with picnic tables and fire grates, $14 per night, drinking water, restrooms with flush toilets, dump station. Pets welcome. The campground can accommodate trailers up to 19 feet and motor homes up to 24 feet. There is a 14-day stay limit. Reservations are accepted and can be made online at recreation.gov or by calling 877-444-6777.

Cottonwood Campground

Located 22 miles south of Santa Elena Junction off Ross Maxwell Scenic Drive. Open year-round, 24 sites with picnic tables and fire grates, $14 per night, drinking water, pit toilets. Pets welcome. There is a 14-day stay limit. Sites are available on a first-come, first-served basis; reservations are not accepted.

Rio Grande Village Campground

Located about 20 miles southeast of the park headquarters. Open year-round, 100 sites with picnic tables and fire grates, $14 per night, drinking water, restrooms with flush toilets, dump station. Pets welcome. The campground can accommodate RVs up to 40 feet. There is a 14-day stay limit. Reservations are accepted and can be made online at recreation.gov or by calling 877-444-6777.

Rio Grande Village RV Campground

Concession-operated RV park located near the Rio Grande Village Visitor Center. Open year-round, 24 sites with full hookups, $33 per night, drinking water, restrooms with flush toilets. Pets welcome. The campground can accommodate RVs up to 40 feet. There is a 14-day stay limit. Reservations are accepted and can be made online at chisosmountainslodge.com or by calling 877-386-4383 or 432-477-2291. The campground is basically a parking lot with spaces for motor homes and trailers.

PARK DETAILS

Guadalupe Mountains National Park

400 Pine Canyon Rd
Salt Flat, TX 79847
Phone: 915-828-3251

Description

Guadalupe Mountains National Park was established in 1972. It protects over 86,000 acres of mountains and canyons and contains the highest point in Texas, 8,749-foot Guadalupe Peak. Visitors can also see a one-room school house and enjoy a picnic on the grounds of Frijole Ranch, located near the park's visitor center. The park also features more than 80 miles of trails that meander through much of the park's wilderness area. On average, nearly 200,000 visitors come to the park annually to enjoy the backpacking, hiking, and camping opportunities.

Information

Information is available from the visitor center located just inside the park off US-62/US-180. The visitor center is open daily all year from 8am to 4:30pm; is closes Christmas Day. Features include extensive natural history exhibits on the park fauna, flora, and geology; a short video is available for viewing.

Fees & Season

The park is open year-round. An entrance fee of $7 per person is charged and is valid for seven days.

Directions

Guadalupe Mountains National Park is located in west Texas about 110 miles east of El Paso via US-62. The northern portion of the park is accessed from New Mexico's State Route 137 about 67 miles southwest of Carlsbad.

RV CAMPING

Dog Canyon Campground

Located on the north side of the park. Open all year, four RV sites with picnic tables, $8 per night, drinking water, restrooms with flush toilets. Pets welcome. The campground can accommodate RVs up to 23 feet. There is a 14-day stay limit. Sites are available on a first-come, first-served basis; reservations are not accepted.

Pine Springs Campground

Located near the visitor center off US-62/US-180. Open year-round, 19 RV sites, $8 per night, drinking water, restrooms with flush toilets. Pets welcome. There is a 14-day stay limit. Sites are available on a first-come, first-served basis; reservations are not accepted. The RV camping area is a paved parking lot with spaces marked for motor homes and trailers. RV fresh water tanks can be filled from a water faucet near the registration board.

PARK DETAILS

Lake Meredith National Recreation Area

PO Box 1460
Fritch, TX 79036
Phone: 806-857-3151

Description

Lake Meredith is an 8,382-acre lake on the Canadian River in the Texas panhandle region. The recreation area was established in 1965. Around 600,000 people come to the park annually to enjoy the boating, fishing, and camping that the park offers. The park also features ranger-guided kayak trips in Spring Canyon throughout the summer and fall, weather permitting.

Information

Information is available from the park headquarters at 419 East Broadway in Fritch. The office is open year-round from 8:00am to 4:30pm, Monday through Friday.

Fees & Season

The park typically remains open year-round. There is no entrance fee charged.

Directions

Lake Meredith National Recreation Area is in northern Texas about 40 miles northeast of Amarillo via SR-136.

RV CAMPING

Blue West Campground

Located about 17 miles west of Sanford via Farm-To-Market Roads 3395 and 1913. Open all year, sites with picnic tables and grills, free. There isn't any drinking water and no flush toilets, vault toilets only. Pets welcome. There is a 14-day stay limit. Sites are available on a first-come, first-served basis; reservations are not accepted.

Fritch Fortress Campground

Located about 3.5 miles north of Fritch on Fritch Fortress Road. Open all year, sites with picnic tables and grills, free, drinking water, restrooms with flush toilets, dump station. Pets welcome. There is a 14-day stay limit. Sites are available on a first-come, first-served basis; reservations are not accepted.

Sanford-Yake Campground

Located near the dam on Sanford-Yake Road. Open all year, 51 sites with picnic tables and grills, free, drinking water, restrooms with flush toilets, showers, dump station nearby. Pets welcome. There is a 14-day stay limit. Sites are available on a first-come, first-served basis; reservations are not accepted. There are 10 RV sites with water and electric hookups (20/30/50 amp) that can be reserved by calling 806-865-3131.

PARK DETAILS

Padre Island National Seashore

PO Box 181300
Corpus Christi, TX 78480
Phone: 361-949-8068

Description

Padre Island National Seashore was established in 1962 and protects over 133,000 acres of barrier island. It is the longest stretch of undeveloped barrier island in the world. Every year from mid-June through August, people come to the park to watch newly hatched sea turtles make their way to the Gulf. More than 500,000 people visit the park each year. The park is sometimes confused with South Padre Island, which is a resort community located near Brownsville, Texas, with numerous hotels, clubs, and beaches. The two destinations are at opposite ends of the barrier island, about 100 miles apart.

Information

Information is available from the Malaquite Beach Visitor Center, open daily from 9am to 5pm throughout the year except Christmas Day. Exhibits detail the park's natural history, plants, and animals. A small museum displays the island's human and natural history. Books and souvenirs are available for purchase, too.

Fees & Season

The park is open all year. An entrance fee of $20 per vehicle is charged and is valid for seven days. A one-day pass can also be purchased for $10 per vehicle.

Directions

Padre Island National Seashore is in southern Texas, southeast of Corpus Christi. The park is reached from I-37 via SR-358.

RV CAMPING

Bird Island Basin Camping Area

Located on the bay side of the island about four miles northwest of the visitor center. Open all year, 34 sites, $8 per night, vault toilets. Pets welcome. There is a 14-day stay limit. Sites are available on a first-come, first-served basis; reservations are not accepted.

Malaquite Campground

Located about one-half mile from the park's visitor center. Open all year, 48 sites with picnic tables, $14 per night, potable water, restrooms with flush toilets, cold showers, dump station nearby. Pets welcome. There is a 14-day stay limit. Sites are available on a first-come, first-served basis; reservations are not accepted.

Utah

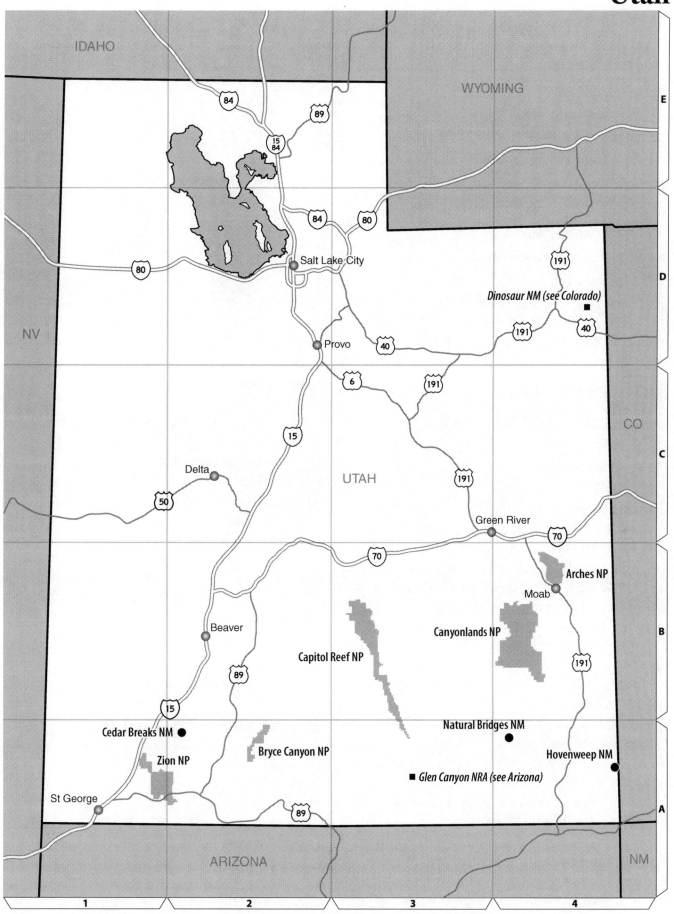

Utah Parks

	Map	Auto Touring	Biking	Boating	Climbing	Fishing	Hiking	Horseback Riding	Hunting	Snow Skiing	Swimming	Visitor Center	Wildlife Viewing
Arches National Park	B4	•	•		•		•					•	•
Bryce Canyon National Park	A2	•	•				•	•				•	•
Canyonlands National Park	B4	•	•	•	•		•	•				•	
Capitol Reef National Park	B3	•	•		•	•	•		•			•	•
Cedar Breaks National Monument	A2	•					•					•	
Dinosaur National Monument - *see Colorado*	D4	•	•			•	•	•				•	•
Glen Canyon National Recreation Area - *see Arizona*	A3	•	•	•			•	•			•	•	•
Hovenweep National Monument	A4						•					•	
Natural Bridges National Monument	A4	•					•					•	
Zion National Park	A1					•		•	•		•		•

PARK DETAILS

Arches National Park

PO Box 907
Moab, UT 84532
Phone: 435-719-2299

Description

Arches National Park features over 2,000 natural stone arches in addition to hundreds of pinnacles, massive fins, and giant balanced rocks. Ranger-led programs occur daily from spring through fall. More than one million visitors come to the park each year for the camping, biking, and rock climbing opportunities. The park receives most visitors between March and October.

Information

Information is available from the park's visitor center located near the park entrance off US-191. The visitor center is open daily all year except Christmas. Hours are typically 9am to 4pm but do vary by the season. Features include a museum with exhibits about the park's natural and cultural history.

Fees & Season

The park remains open year-round. An entrance fee of $30 is charged and is valid for seven days.

Directions

Arches National Park is in southeast Utah five miles north of Moab along US-191.

RV CAMPING

Devils Garden Campground

Located about 18 miles from the park entrance. Open all year, 50 sites with picnic tables and fire grates, $25 per night, drinking water, restrooms with flush toilets, pit toilets. Pets welcome. The campground can accommodate RVs up to 40 feet. There is a 14-day stay limit. Reservations are required from March through October and can be made online at recreation.gov or by calling 877-444-6777.

PARK DETAILS

Bryce Canyon National Park

PO Box 640201
Bryce, UT 84764
Phone: 435-834-5322

Description

Bryce Canyon National Park was established in 1923. The park protects 35,835 acres of colorful and odd-shaped pillars of rock called hoodoos. Fourteen overlooks along the park's 18-mile main road offer panoramic views of the surrounding landscape. Those interested in exploring more of the park's backcountry will find numerous hiking trails from easy to strenuous. Horseback riding in the park is also popular. Over two million visitors come to the park every year, mostly between March and early October.

Information

Information is available from the park's visitor center located about 1.5 miles from the park entrance. The visitor center is open all year except Thanksgiving, Christmas, and New Year's Day. Summer hours are 8am to 8pm; winter hours are 8am to 4:30pm; fall and spring hours are 8am to 6pm. A museum within the visitor center features geology, wildlife, and historic and prehistoric culture exhibits.

Fees & Season

The park is open all year but there may be temporary road closures during and shortly after winter snow storms. An entrance fee of $35 is charged and is valid for seven days.

Directions

Bryce Canyon National Park is in south-central Utah about 70 miles east of Cedar City via SR-14, US-89, and SR-12. From the north, travelers can take I-15 Exit 95 and follow SR-20 east to US-89; go south to SR-12 and go east to SR-63, which leads into the park.

RV CAMPING

North Campground

Located near the park's visitor center. Open all year, 52 RV sites with picnic tables and fire grates, $30 per night, drinking water, restrooms with flush toilets, dump station (summer only - fee charged). Coin-operated laundry and shower facilities are available at the general store nearby. Pets welcome. The campground can accommodate RVs up to 30 feet. There is a 14-day stay limit. Reservations are accepted and can be made online at recreation.gov or by calling 877-444-6777. Sites typically fill by early afternoon during the summer months.

Sunset Campground

Located about 1.5 miles south of the visitor center. Open late spring to early fall, 49 RV sites with picnic tables and fire grates, $30 per night, drinking water, restrooms with flush toilets. Pets welcome. The campground can accommodate RVs up to 45 feet. There is a 14-day stay limit. Sites are available on a first-come, first-served basis; reservations are not accepted for RV sites. Sites typically fill by early afternoon.

PARK DETAILS

Canyonlands National Park

2282 SW Resource Blvd
Moab, UT 84532
Phone: 435-719-2313

Description

Canyonlands National Park preserves 337,598 acres of colorful canyons, mesas, buttes, fins, arches, and spires in the heart of southeast Utah's high desert. The park is comprised of four districts. The Island in the Sky is closest to Moab and is the most visited district. The paved road in this district has numerous overlooks for viewing the expansive landscape. The Needles is in the southern portion of the park about 75 miles from Moab and offers more of a backcountry experience. The Maze is a remote district requiring considerably more time and self-reliance to visit. The Horseshoe Unit is northwest of The Maze and is detached from the rest of the park. It contains significant rock art including life-sized figures with intricate designs.

Information

Information is available from two visitor centers. Island in the Sky Visitor Center is in the park's northern unit, 32 miles from Moab via US-191 and SR-313. The visitor center is generally open daily from March through December (closed Christmas Day). In January and February, the visitor center is open Friday through Tuesday (closed Wednesday and Thursday). Hours are typically 8am to 5pm but vary by season.

The Needles Visitor Center is in the southern part of the park and is 76 miles from Moab via US 191 and SR-211. It is typically open early March to late November from 9am to 4pm. Needles closes over the winter but bathrooms and water is available year-round. Both visitor centers feature exhibits of the area's natural and cultural history.

Fees & Season

The park remains open year-round. An entrance fee of $30 is charged and is valid for seven days.

Directions

Canyonlands National Park is located in southeast Utah, southwest of Moab. From US-191 north of Moab, SR-313 leads to the Island in the Sky district. From US-191 south of Moab, SR-211 leads to The Needles district. The Maze district is only accessible from unpaved roads that typically require a high-clearance, four-wheel-drive vehicle to reach. Roads may become impassable when wet. Horseshoe Canyon Unit is 32 miles east of SR-24 via unpaved roads that are accessible to two-wheel-drive vehicles but may become impassable when wet.

RV CAMPING

Squaw Flat Campground

Located in The Needles district about 3.5 miles west of the visitor center. Open year-round, 26 sites with picnic tables and fire grates, $20 per night, drinking water (seasonal), restrooms with flush toilets (seasonally, vault toilets available year-round). Pets welcome. The campground can accommodate RVs up to 28 feet. There is a 7-day stay limit. Reservations are accepted and can be made online at recreation.gov or by calling 877-444-6777. Sites fill quickly in spring and fall.

Willow Flat Campground

Located in the Island in the Sky district about 7.5 miles southwest of the visitor center. Open year-round, 12 sites with picnic tables and fire grates, $15 per night, vault toilets. Pets welcome. The campground can accommodate RVs up to 28 feet. There is a 7-day stay limit. Sites are available on a first-come, first-served basis; reservations are not accepted. Sites fill quickly spring through fall.

PARK DETAILS

Capitol Reef National Park

HC 70 Box 15
Torrey, UT 84775
Phone: 435-425-3791

Description

Capitol Reef became a national monument in 1937. Its boundaries were later changed and Capitol Reef became a national park in 1971. Today the park protects 243,921 acres and features geologic landforms of the Waterpocket Fold and Cathedral Valley. Archeological evidence of prehistoric American Indians and elements of a historic Mormon settlement are also preserved. Fifteen day hiking trails are located in the Fruita area ranging in length from a quarter mile to ten miles. Backcountry hiking is also a popular activity. The park is designated an International Dark-Sky Park.

Information

Information is available from the Capitol Reef Visitor Center located ten miles east of Torrey off SR-24. It is open daily from 8am to 4:30pm with extended hours spring through fall; it closes on Christmas Day. A museum offers an overview of the park's features and exhibits on geology, archeology, and history.

Fees & Season

The park remains open all year. An entrance fee of $20 per vehicle, good for seven days, is charged to tour the park's scenic drive beyond the Fruita Campground.

Directions

Capitol Reef National Park is in south-central Utah about 160 miles northeast of Cedar City. SR-24 passes through the park and can be accessed from Interstate 70 at Exit 149 near Green River and at Exit 48 near Sigurd.

RV CAMPING

Fruita Campground

Located near the park's visitor center. Open all year, 64 sites with picnic tables and fire grates, $20 per night, drinking water, restrooms with flush toilets, dump station. Pets welcome. The campground can accommodate large RVs. There is a 14-day stay limit. Reservations are accepted and can be made online at recreation.gov or by calling 877-444-6777.

PARK DETAILS

Cedar Breaks National Monument

2390 W Hwy 56, Suite 11
Cedar City, UT 84720
Phone: 435-586-9451 x4420

Description
Cedar Breaks National Monument preserves a huge natural amphitheater that has been eroded out of the multicolored Pink Cliffs. The canyon spans some three miles and is over 2,000 feet deep. Visitation has increased in recent years; nearly one million people now visit the park annually.

Information
Information is available from the Cedar Breaks Visitor Center on SR-148. The visitor center is open daily from late May to mid-October; hours are 9am to 6pm. A two-mile hiking trail begins here that will take you to some panoramic overlooks.

Fees & Season
The park remains open year-round but SR-148 closes after the first heavy snowfall, which is usually in mid-November. An entrance fee of $7 per person is charged and is valid for seven days.

Directions
Cedar Breaks National Monument is about 22 miles east of Interstate 15 Exit 59 in Cedar City via SR-14 and SR-148.

RV CAMPING

Point Supreme Campground
Located near the park's visitor center along SR-148. Open mid-June to late September, 25 sites with picnic tables and fire grates, $24 per night, drinking water, restrooms with flush toilets, showers. Pets welcome.

The campground can accommodate RVs up to 35 feet at some sites. There is a 7-day stay limit. Reservations are accepted and can be made online at recreation.gov or by calling 877-444-6777. Opening and closing dates are weather dependant.

PARK DETAILS

Hovenweep National Monument

McElmo Route
Cortez, CO 81321
Phone: 970-562-4282 x5

Description
Hovenweep National Monument was established in 1923. It protects six ancestral Pueblo villages spread over a large area along the Utah-Colorado border. The Square Tower Unit is the largest section of the monument and contains the most extensive archeological remains. The remote park is not very well known. On average, the park receives about 30,000 visitors annually. Most come in the spring or fall.

Information
Information is available from the visitor center located in the Square Tower Unit (see directions below). The visitor center is open all year. Hours are typically 9am to 5pm but may change depending on the season, staffing, and holidays. In winter, the visitor center is closed on Tuesdays and Wednesdays in addition to winter holidays.

Fees & Season
The park remains open year-round. An entrance fee of $15 per vehicle is charged.

Directions
Hovenweep National Monument is located along the border of southeast Utah and southwest Colorado. From Blanding, Utah, follow US-191 south about 15 miles; turn left to go east on SR-262 for eight miles; turn left and continue eastward on Hovenweep Road for 6.7 miles; turn right onto Reservation Road and follow for 9.4 miles; turn left to stay on Reservation Road and continue for about 6 miles to park entrance.

RV CAMPING

Hovenweep Campground

Located near the visitor center. Open year-round, 16 sites with picnic tables and fire grates, $15 per night, restrooms with flush toilets. Drinking water is available during warmer months; there is a five gallon limit per person. A water spigot at the visitor center is available year-round. Pets welcome. The campground can accommodate RVs up to 36 feet. There is a 14-day stay limit. Sites are available on a first-come, first-served basis; reservations are not accepted. Rates are reduced during winter, from November through February.

PARK DETAILS

Natural Bridges National Monument

HC 60 Box 1
Lake Powell, UT 84533
Phone: 435-692-1234

Description

Natural Bridges National Monument features three bridges naturally carved out of sandstone. The one-way loop road through the park has numerous overlooks for viewing the natural bridges and surrounding landscape. The bridges are named "Kachina," "Owachomo" and "Sipapu" in honor of the Native Americans that once made this area their home. The park also features ancient Indian rock art and ruins. It was established in 1908 and encompasses 7,636 acres. More than 100,000 people come to this park every year. Natural Bridges was the world's first International Dark-Sky Park.

Information

Information is available from the Natural Bridges Visitor Center located near the park entrance. The visitor center remains open all year except on winter holidays. Hours are typically 9am to 5pm but may change depending on the season, staffing, and holidays. In winter, the visitor center is closed on Tuesdays and Wednesdays. An orientation video is shown on request. Exhibits highlight the natural and cultural history of the area.

Fees & Season

The park remains open all year but roads may temporarily close in winter after snowfall while crews plow. An entrance fee of $20 per vehicle is charged and is valid for seven days. Use of a credit card is the park's preferred payment method.

Directions

Natural Bridges National Monument is in southeast Utah about 40 miles west of Blanding via SR-95 and SR-275.

RV CAMPING

Natural Bridges Campground

Located 1/4 mile west of the park visitor center. Open year-round, 13 sites with picnic tables and fire grates, $15 per night, vault toilets. Water and restrooms with flush toilets are available at the nearby visitor center. Pets welcome. The campground can accommodate RVs up to 26 feet. There is a 7-day stay limit from mid-April to mid-October; 14 days otherwise. Sites are available on a first-come, first-served basis; reservations are not accepted. The campground usually fills by early afternoon from March through October. Rates are reduced November through February.

PARK DETAILS

Zion National Park

1 Zion Park Blvd
State Route 9
Springdale, UT 84767
Phone: 435-772-3256

Description

Zion National Park protects over 143,000 acres of massive, colorful sandstone cliffs and narrow canyons. The park was established in 1919 and is visited by more than four million people each year. The southern portion is the most visited part of the park; the developed campgrounds are located here as is Zion Canyon and the Angels Landing Trail. Shuttle busses run spring through fall in Zion Canyon. The Kolob

Canyons section is the northwest portion of the park. It features a five-mile route with several scenic overlooks and access to hiking trails.

Information

Information is available from two visitor centers. Zion Canyon Visitor Center is open daily year-round except Christmas. Summer hours are typically 8am to 7pm; hours vary the rest of the year. It is located just beyond the park's entrance on SR-9. Kolob Canyons Visitor Center is open daily year-round except Thanksgiving and Christmas. It is located just east of I-15 Exit 40. Hours vary by season.

Fees & Season

The park is open all year. An entrance fee of $35 per vehicle is charged and is valid for seven days. A $15 fee is charged for large vehicles to safely pass through the Zion-Mount Carmel Tunnel. Park rangers posted at both ends of the tunnel convert the two-way tunnel traffic to one-way for large vehicles. Have your vehicle measured and pay the fee at the entrance station. Any vehicle that is 7 feet 10 inches wide and/or 11 feet 4 inches in height or larger is required to have a tunnel permit. Vehicles over 13 feet 1 inch tall, single vehicles over 40 feet long, or combined vehicles over 50 feet long are prohibited from passing through the tunnel.

Directions

Zion National Park is in southwest Utah about 40 miles northeast of Saint George. The park can be reached from I-15 Exit 16 by traveling east on SR-9.

RV CAMPING

South Campground

Located 1/2 mile from the park's southern entrance along SR-9. Open March to November, 51 RV sites with picnic tables and fire grates, $20 per night, drinking water, restrooms with flush toilets, dump station. Pets welcome. There is a 14-day stay limit. Reservations are accepted and can be made online at recreation.gov or by calling 877-444-6777.

Watchman Campground

Located 1/4 mile from the park's southern entrance off SR-9. Open year-round, 90 sites with electric hookups, picnic tables and fire grates, $30 per night, drinking water, restrooms with flush toilets, dump station. Pets welcome. There is a 14-day stay limit. Reservations are accepted and can be made online at recreation.gov or by calling 877-444-6777. Sites are available on a first-come, first-served basis from December through February.

Virginia

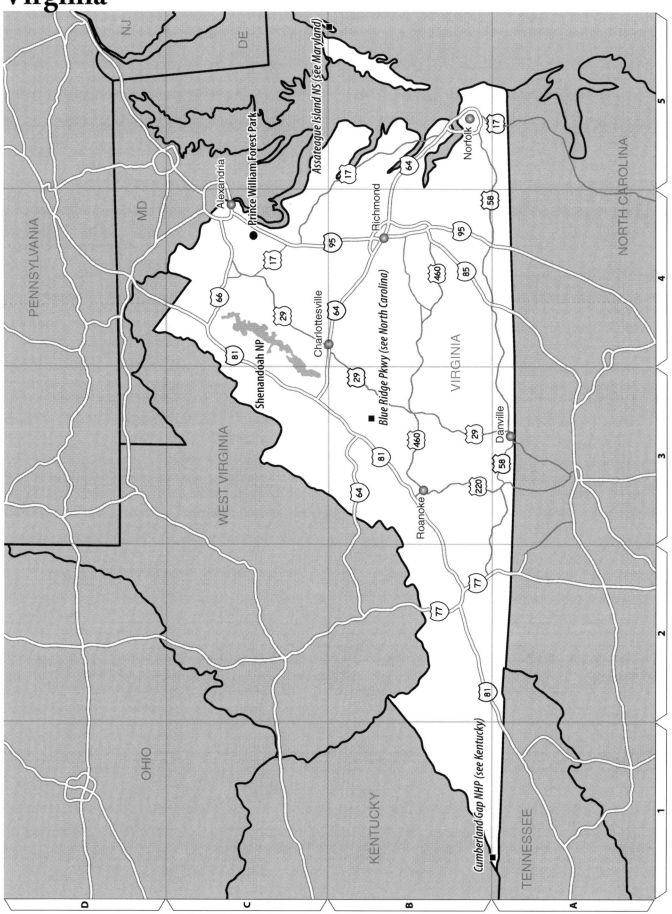

Virginia Parks

	Map	Auto Touring	Biking	Boating	Climbing	Fishing	Hiking	Horseback Riding	Hunting	Snow Skiing	Swimming	Visitor Center	Wildlife Viewing
Assateague Island National Seashore - *see Maryland*	B5		•	•		•	•	•	•		•	•	•
Blue Ridge Parkway - *see North Carolina*	B3	•	•	•		•	•	•			•	•	•
Cumberland Gap National Historical Park - *see Kentucky*	A1	•	•				•		•			•	•
Prince William Forest Park	C4	•	•			•	•					•	•
Shenandoah National Park	C4	•	•		•	•	•		•			•	•

PARK DETAILS

Prince William Forest Park

18100 Park Headquarters Road
Triangle, VA 22172
Phone: 703-221-7181

Description

Prince William Forest was established in 1935 as the Chopawamsic Recreation Demonstration Area. The park's land was set aside during the Great Depression and in 1935 the Civilian Conservation Corps began restoring the previously over-farmed land, converting it to recreational lands for public use. The CCC built trails, dams, and cabins. It was renamed in 1948. Today, the park protects over 15,000 acres of pine and hardwood forests. More than 300,000 people come to the park each year to enjoy the camping, hiking, picnicking, and bicycling opportunities.

Information

Information is available from the visitor center located about 1/2 mile from the park's entrance. The visitor center is open daily year-round except Thanksgiving, Christmas, and New Year's Day. Hours are 9am to 5pm, March through October, and 8am to 4pm, November through February. Exhibits feature the park's historic and natural resources. A video is shown on request.

Fees & Season

The park is open all year. An entrance fee of $7 per vehicle is charged and is valid for seven days.

Directions

Prince William Forest Park is in northeast Virginia about 30 miles southwest of Arlington. The park is accessible from I-95 at Exit 150.

RV CAMPING

Oak Ridge Campground

Located in the western portion of the park about 6.5 miles from the visitor center. Open March through November, 67 RV sites with picnic tables and fire grates, $26 per night, drinking water, restrooms with flush toilets, showers in Loop B. Pets welcome. The campground can accommodate trailers up to 26 feet and motor homes up to 32 feet. There is a 14-day stay limit. Reservations are required for sites in Loop B from April through October and can be made online at recreation.gov or by calling 877-444-6777.

Prince William Forest RV Campground

Concession-operated campground located along Dumfries Road about 2.5 miles west of I-95 Exit 152B. Open all year, 36 sites with water and electric, 36 full-hookup sites, $37 per night for water and electric sites with 30-amp service, $40 per night for full hookup sites with 30-amp service, $55 per night for full hookup sites with 50-amp service, picnic tables, fire pits, drinking water, restrooms with flush toilets, showers, dump station, coin-operated laundry, swimming pool, playground. Pets welcome. The campground can accommodate large RVs at some sites. There is a 14-day stay limit. Reservations are accepted and can be made by calling 888-737-5730. For general campground information, call 703-221-2474.

PARK DETAILS

Shenandoah National Park

3655 US Highway 211E
Luray, VA 22835
Phone: 540-999-3500

Description

Established in 1935, Shenandoah National Park protects over 200,000 acres of the Blue Ridge Mountains in northern Virginia. The park features over 500 miles of hiking trails, including 101 miles of the Appalachian Trail. Some trails lead to a waterfall or viewpoint while others wind deep into the forests and wilderness. Visitors can drive the scenic 105-mile Skyline Drive, which winds along the crest of the mountains and offers stunning views from any of the 75 scenic overlooks. RVers need to be certain they will clear Marys Rock Tunnel (just south of Thornton Gap entrance from US-211) at 12 feet 8 inches. Nearly 1.5 million people visit the park annually.

Information

Information is available from two visitor centers within the park. Dickey Ridge Visitor Center is located at Mile 4.6 on Skyline Drive and has restrooms, exhibits, an orientation movie, and a bookstore. It is typically open daily between 9am and 5pm from April to late November. Another visitor center is located at Mile 51 on Skyline Drive with information, restrooms, exhibits, videos, and publications. The Byrd Visitor Center is usually open daily between 9am and 5pm from late March to late November.

Fees & Season

The park is open all year, however, portions of Skyline Drive are periodically closed during inclement weather and at night during deer hunting season (mid-November through early January). An entrance fee of $30 per vehicle is charged and is valid for seven days.

Directions

Shenandoah National Park is located in the Blue Ridge Mountains about 70 miles west of Washington, D.C. and stretches 105 miles from its northern entrance at Front Royal to its southern entrance near Waynesboro. US-33 and US-211 cross the park and also provide access to Skyline Drive.

RV CAMPING

Big Meadows Campground

Located near the Byrd Visitor Center at Mile 51.2 on Skyline Drive. Open late March to mid-November, 168 sites with picnic tables and fire grates, $20 per night, drinking water, restrooms with flush toilets, dump station, coin-operated showers and laundry facility. Pets welcome. The campground can accommodate large RVs at some sites. There is a 14-day stay limit. Reservations are accepted and can be made online at recreation.gov or by calling 877-444-6777. Three waterfalls are within walking distance.

Lewis Mountain Campground

Located at Mile 57.5 on Skyline Drive. Open April through October, 31 sites with picnic tables and fire grates, $15 per night, drinking water, restrooms with flush toilets. Pets welcome. There is a 30-day stay limit. Sites are available on a first-come, first-served basis; reservations are not accepted.

Loft Mountain Campground

Located at Mile 79.5 on Skyline Drive. Open May to late October, 155 sites with picnic tables and fire grates, $15 per night, drinking water, restrooms with flush toilets, dump station. Camp store with showers and laundry nearby. Pets welcome. The campground can accommodate large RVs at some sites. There is a 14-day stay limit. Reservations are accepted and can be made online at recreation.gov or by calling 877-444-6777. Two waterfalls and trails into Big Run Wilderness are nearby.

Mathews Arm Campground

Located at Mile 22.2 on Skyline Drive. Open May to late October, 161 sites with picnic tables and fire grates, $15 per night, drinking water, restrooms with flush toilets, dump station. Pets welcome. The campground can accommodate large RVs at some sites. There is a 30-day stay limit. Reservations are accepted and can be made online at recreation.gov or by calling 877-444-6777. A trail from the campground leads to the park's tallest waterfall, the Overall Run Falls.

Washington

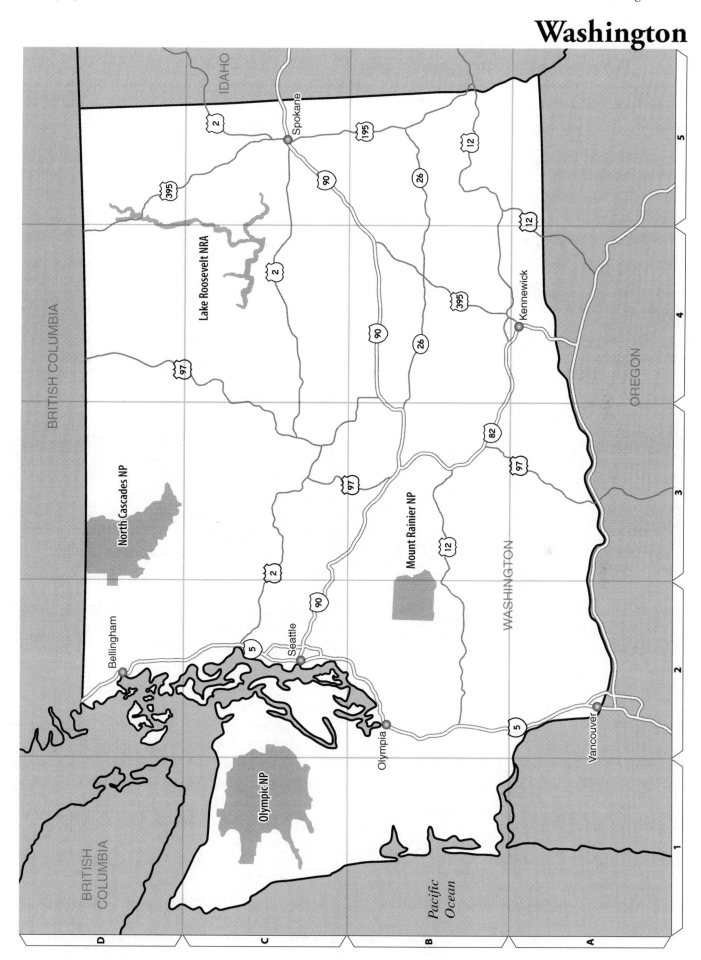

Washington Parks

	Map	Auto Touring	Biking	Boating	Climbing	Fishing	Hiking	Horseback Riding	Hunting	Snow Skiing	Swimming	Visitor Center	Wildlife Viewing
Lake Roosevelt National Recreation Area	C4	•		•		•	•		•			•	•	•
Mount Rainier National Park	B2	•	•		•	•	•	•			•		•	•
North Cascades National Park	D3	•	•	•	•	•	•						•	•
Olympic National Park	C1	•	•	•	•	•	•	•		•	•	•	•	•

PARK DETAILS

Lake Roosevelt National Recreation Area

1008 Crest Dr
Coulee Dam, WA 99116
Phone: 509-754-7800

Description

In 1941 the Grand Coulee Dam was built on the Columbia River, creating a 130-mile long lake. Named for President Franklin D. Roosevelt, the recreation area provides opportunities for boating, fishing, swimming, and camping. The park also features the historic Fort Spokane, one of the final military forts built in the Western Frontier, and the remains of Saint Paul's Mission in Kettle Falls. More than one million visitors come to the park annually.

Information

Information is available from the Fort Spokane Visitor Center and Museum on SR-25 about 21 miles north of Davenport. From Memorial Day to Labor Day, the hours are 9:30am to 5pm; it is open by request the rest of the year. Exhibits focus on the natural history of the area, daily life in the military, Indian boarding school, and Indian hospital periods.

Fees & Season

The park is open all year. Lake levels can vary by season, which can lead to the closure of boat launches and the loss of water pressure in some campgrounds. An entrance fee is not charged.

Directions

Lake Roosevelt National Recreation Area is in northeast Washington between Coulee Dam and Kettle Falls. Access to the park is by way of several roads but primarily SR-21, SR-25, SR-155, and SR-174.

RV CAMPING

Evans Campground

Located about ten miles north of Kettle Falls on SR-25. Open all year, 36 sites with picnic tables and fire grates, $18 per night May through September, $9 per night October through April, drinking water (seasonal), restrooms with flush toilets (seasonal), vault toilets, dump station, swimming beach. Pets welcome. The campground can accommodate large RVs at some sites. There is a 14-day stay limit. Sites are available on a first-come, first-served basis; reservations are not accepted. The campground is busy in summer and tends to fill on the weekends.

Fort Spokane Campground

Located near the Fort Spokane Visitor Center on SR-25 about 24 miles north of Davenport. Open all year, 63 sites with picnic tables and fire grates, $18 per night May through September, $9 per night October through April, drinking water (seasonal), restrooms with flush toilets (seasonal), vault toilets, dump station, swimming beach. Pets welcome. The campground can accommodate large RVs at some sites. There is a 14-day stay limit. Reservations are accepted and can be made online at recreation.gov or by calling 877-444-6777.

Gifford Campground

Located about 25 miles south of Kettle Falls off SR-25. Open all year, 42 sites with picnic tables and fire grates, $18 per night May through September, $9 per night

October through April, drinking water (seasonal), restrooms with flush toilets (seasonal), vault toilets, dump station. Pets welcome. The campground can accommodate large RVs at some sites. There is a 14-day stay limit. Sites are available on a first-come, first-served basis; reservations are not accepted.

Haag Cove Campground

Located about ten miles southwest of Kettle Falls via US-395, SR-20, and CR-3. Open all year, 12 sites with picnic tables and fire grates, $18 per night May through September, $9 per night October through April, drinking water (seasonal), vault toilets. Pets welcome. The campground can accommodate large RVs at some sites. There is a 14-day stay limit. Sites are available on a first-come, first-served basis; reservations are not accepted. The campground is typically quiet but may fill on holidays and weekends in summer.

Hawk Creek Campground

Located about 14 miles northeast of Creston via US-2 and Miles Creston Road. Open all year, 20 sites with picnic tables and fire grates, $18 per night May through September, $9 per night October through April, drinking water (seasonal), vault toilets. Pets welcome. The campground can accommodate large RVs at some sites. There is a 14-day stay limit. Sites are available on a first-come, first-served basis; reservations are not accepted.

Hunters Campground

Located one mile west of SR-25 in Hunters. Open all year, 37 sites with picnic tables and fire grates, $18 per night May through September, $9 per night October through April, drinking water (seasonal), restrooms with flush toilets (seasonal), vault toilets, dump station, swimming beach. Pets welcome. The campground can accommodate large RVs at some sites. There is a 14-day stay limit. Sites are available on a first-come, first-served basis; reservations are not accepted. The campground is very popular and often busy in the summer.

Jones Bay Campground

Located 18 miles north of Wilbur via SR-21 and Eftner Road. Open all year, 9 sites with picnic tables and fire grates, $18 per night May through September, $9 per night October through April, drinking water (seasonal), vault toilets. Pets welcome. The campground can accommodate large RVs at some sites. There is a 14-day stay limit. Sites are available on a first-come, first-served basis; reservations are not accepted.

Kamloops Island Campground

Located off US-395 about 7 miles northwest of Kettle Falls. Open all year, 17 sites with picnic tables and fire grates, $18 per night May through September, $9 per night October through April, drinking water (seasonal), vault toilets. Pets welcome. The campground can accommodate large RVs at some sites. There is a 14-day stay limit. Sites are available on a first-come, first-served basis; reservations are not accepted.

Keller Ferry Campground

Concession-managed campground about 15 miles north of Wilbur via SR-21. Open all year, 44 sites with picnic tables and fire grates, $18 per night, drinking water (seasonal), restrooms with flush toilets (seasonal), vault toilets, dump station, swimming beach. Pets welcome. The campground can accommodate large RVs at some sites. There is a 14-day stay limit. Reservations are accepted and can be made online at lakerooseveltadventures.com or by calling 509-647-5755.

Kettle Falls Campground

Located about five miles southwest of Kettle Falls via US-395 and Boise-Cascade Road. Open all year, 76 sites with picnic tables and fire grates, $18 per night May through September, $9 per night October through April, drinking water (seasonal), restrooms with flush toilets (seasonal), vault toilets, dump station, swimming beach. Pets welcome. The campground can accommodate large RVs at some sites. There is a 14-day stay limit. Reservations are accepted and can be made online at recreation.gov or by calling 877-444-6777.

Kettle River Campground

Located about 9.5 miles northwest of Kettle Falls via US-395. Open all year, 13 sites with picnic tables and fire grates, $18 per night May through September, $9 per night October through April, drinking water (seasonal), vault toilets. Pets welcome. The campground can accommodate large RVs at some sites. There is a 14-day stay limit. Sites are available on a first-come, first-served basis; reservations are not accepted. The campground is typically quiet and doesn't often fill.

RV Camping in National Parks

Marcus Island Campground

Located about 6.5 miles north of Kettle Falls via SR-25. Open all year, 25 sites with picnic tables and fire grates, $18 per night May through September, $9 per night October through April, drinking water (seasonal), vault toilets, swimming beach. Pets welcome. The campground can accommodate large RVs at some sites. There is a 14-day stay limit. Sites are available on a first-come, first-served basis; reservations are not accepted.

North Gorge Campground

Located about 17 miles north of Kettle Falls via SR-25. Open all year, 6 RV sites with picnic tables and fire grates, $18 per night May through September, $9 per night October through April, drinking water (seasonal), vault toilets. Pets welcome. The campground can accommodate large RVs at some sites. There is a 14-day stay limit. Sites are available on a first-come, first-served basis; reservations are not accepted. The small campground is popular and busy on summer weekends.

Snag Cove Campground

Located about 13 miles north of Kettle Falls via US-395 and Northport Flat Creek Rd. Open all year, 9 sites with picnic tables and fire grates, $18 per night May through September, $9 per night October through April, drinking water (seasonal), vault toilets. Pets welcome. The campground can accommodate large RVs at some sites. There is a 14-day stay limit. Sites are available on a first-come, first-served basis; reservations are not accepted. Because of its size and popularity, Snag Cove often fills in the summer.

Spring Canyon Campground

Located three miles east of Grand Coulee via SR-174. Open all year, 78 sites with picnic tables and fire grates, $18 per night May through September, $9 per night October through April, drinking water (seasonal), restrooms with flush toilets (seasonal), vault toilets, dump station, swimming beach. Pets welcome. The campground can accommodate large RVs at some sites. There is a 14-day stay limit. Reservations are accepted and can be made online at recreation.gov or by calling 877-444-6777.

PARK DETAILS

Mount Rainier National Park

55210 238th Ave E
Ashford, WA 98304
Phone: 360-569-2211

Description

Mount Rainier National Park was established in 1899. It features the 14,410 foot high Mount Rainier, an active volcano, and encompasses more than 235,000 acres. About 97 percent of the park is designated wilderness, which provides opportunities for hiking the back country. Thousands of visitors each year hike the historic 93-mile Wonderland Trail, which circles the mountain. A portion of the Pacific Crest Trail also weaves in and out of the park along the eastern boundary. Over one million people visit the park each year to enjoy the many outdoor activities offered by the park.

Information

Information is available from three visitor centers. Jackson Visitor Center is in Paradise about 18 miles from the park's southwest entrance. It is open 10am to 5pm daily during summer; in winter it is only open on weekends. Features include exhibits of the natural and cultural history of the park. Ohanapecosh Visitor Center is in the southeast corner of the park off SR-123 and is open daily in summer. The Sunrise Visitor Center is open daily in summer and is located in the northeast corner of the park on Sunrise Park Road.

Fees & Season

The park is open all year but vehicle access in winter is from the southwest entrance; visitation is at its peak in July and August. The park is generally less crowded mid-week. Wait times at the Nisqually and White River entrances can be over an hour on the busiest summer weekends and holidays. An entrance fee of $30 per vehicle is charged and is valid for seven days.

Directions

Mount Rainier National Park is in west-central Washington about 60 miles southeast of Olympia. Portions of the park are accessed by SR-410 from the northeast, SR-123 from the southeast, and SR-706 from the southwest.

RV CAMPING

Cougar Rock Campground

Located about 8.5 miles east of the park's Nisqually Entrance (southwest entrance). Open late May to late September, 173 sites with picnic tables and fire grates, $20 per night, drinking water, restrooms with flush toilets, dump station. Pets welcome. The campground can accommodate trailers up to 27 feet and motor homes up to 35 feet. There is a 14-day stay limit. Reservations are accepted and can be made online at recreation.gov or by calling 877-444-6777.

Ohanapecosh Campground

Located near the Ohanapecosh Visitor Center about two miles from the park's southeast entrance on SR-123. Open late May to late September, 188 sites with picnic tables and fire grates, $20 per night, drinking water, restrooms with flush toilets. Pets welcome. The campground can accommodate trailers up to 27 feet and motor homes up to 32 feet. There is a 14-day stay limit. Reservations are accepted and can be made online at recreation.gov or by calling 877-444-6777.

White River Campground

Located about six miles west of SR-410 and the park's White River Entrance (northeast entrance). Open late June to late September, 112 sites with picnic tables and fire grates, $20 per night, drinking water, restrooms with flush toilets. Pets welcome. The campground can accommodate trailers up to 18 feet and motor homes up to 27 feet. There is a 14-day stay limit. Sites are available on a first-come, first-served basis; reservations are not accepted.

PARK DETAILS

North Cascades National Park

810 State Route 20
Sedro-Woolley, WA 98284
Phone: 360-854-7200

Description

North Cascades National Park was established in 1968 and encompasses over 684,000 acres. Within the park are two National Recreation Areas: Lake Chelan and Ross Lake. Most of the park is designated wilderness and is not vehicle-accessible. The RV campgrounds described below are within the Ross Lake National Recreation Area. Lake Chelan National Recreation Area is only accessible by foot or ferry. The park features nearly 400 miles of hiking trails; a part of the Pacific Crest National Scenic Trail crosses the park. On average, fewer than 25,000 people visit the park annually.

Information

Information is available from the North Cascades Visitor Center located along SR-20 near milepost 120 and the town of Newhalem. The visitor center is open daily in summer from 9am to 6pm. It features multimedia exhibits on the park's natural and cultural history. Information is also available from the park's headquarters in Sedro-Woolley along SR-20 about seven miles east of I-5 Exit 230.

Fees & Season

The park is open all year. No entrance fee is charged.

Directions

North Cascades National Park is in northern Washington about 50 miles east of Mount Vernon via SR-20.

RV CAMPING

Colonial Creek Campground

Located off SR-20 near milepost 130 about ten miles east of Newhalem. Open late May to late September (some sites remain open in winter but with no water, services, or fees), 142 sites with picnic tables and fire grates, $16 per night, drinking water, restrooms with flush toilets, dump station. Pets welcome. The campground is not large RV friendly. There is a 14-day stay limit. Reservations are accepted and can be made online at recreation.gov or by calling 877-444-6777.

Goodell Creek Campground

Located south of SR-20 just west of Newhalem. Open year-round, 19 sites with picnic tables and fire grates,

$16 per night, drinking water, vault toilets. No water, services, or fees charged from late September to spring. Pets welcome. The campground is best suited for small RVs. There is a 14-day stay limit. Sites are available on a first-come, first-served basis; reservations are not accepted.

Gorge Lake Campground

Located just outside the town of Diablo, north of SR-20 about 20 miles east of Marblemount. Open year-round, six sites with picnic tables and fire grates, free, vault toilets. No water. Pets welcome. There is a 14-day stay limit. Sites are available on a first-come, first-served basis; reservations are not accepted.

Hozomeen Campground

Located 40 miles south of Hope, British Columbia, in Canada No road access from the United States. Open year-round, 75 sites with picnic tables and fire grates, free, potable water (seasonal), vault toilets. Pets welcome. There is a 14-day stay limit. Sites are available on a first-come, first-served basis; reservations are not accepted.

Newhalem Creek Campground

Located south of SR-20 at milepost 120 about 14 miles east of Marblemount. Open late May to late September, 111 sites with picnic tables and fire grates, $16 per night, drinking water, restrooms with flush toilets, dump station. Pets welcome. The campground can accommodate RVs up to 45 feet at some sites. There is a 14-day stay limit. Reservations are accepted and can be made online at recreation.gov or by calling 877-444-6777.

PARK DETAILS

Olympic National Park

600 E Park Ave
Port Angeles, WA 98362
Phone: 360-565-3130

Description

Olympic National Park was established in 1935 and protects nearly one million acres of old-growth forests and temperate rain forests. Among its features are glacier-capped mountains, valleys, meadows, lakes, and miles of beaches. Over 95% of the park is designated wilderness and is not vehicle-accessible. More than 600 miles of trails lead deeper into the park's wilderness. The park receives over three million visitors every year.

Information

Information is available from three visitor centers. Olympic National Park Visitor Center is located at 3002 Mount Angeles Road in Port Angeles. It is open daily year-round except Thanksgiving and Christmas Day; hours vary according to season. The visitor center features exhibits about the natural and cultural history of the park, an orientation film shown on request, a book store, and two short nature trails.

Hurricane Ridge Visitor Center is located about 17 miles south of Port Angeles. It is generally open daily from late May to mid-October. It features exhibits about the park's mountain habitats and an orientation film. Guided walks and talks are offered during the summer. A snack shop and gift shop are also located on the premises.

Hoh Rain Forest Visitor Center is located about 31 miles south of Forks off US-101. It is open daily in summer from 9am to 5pm and on weekends during the off-season. Hours vary according to season. Features include exhibits about the park's temperate rain forests and self-guided nature trails.

Fees & Season

The park is open all year but some roads and visitor facilities close in winter. An entrance fee of $30 per vehicle is charged and is valid for seven days. A $10 fee is charged for use of dump stations. Camping fees are payable in cash or check only. Many campgrounds are self-registration; change for over payment cannot be made.

Directions

Olympic National Park is in northwest Washington about 100 miles northwest of Olympia. Various portions of the park are accessible from points along US-101.

RV CAMPING

Fairholme Campground

Located 26 miles west of Port Angeles on US-101. Open May through September, 88 sites with picnic tables and fire grates, $20 per night, drinking water, restrooms with flush toilets, dump station. Pets welcome. The campground can accommodate RVs up to 21 feet. There is a 14-day stay limit. Sites are available on a first-come, first-served basis; reservations are not accepted.

Heart O' the Hills Campground

Located five miles south of Port Angeles along Hurricane Ridge Road. Open year-round (walk-in only if snow-covered), 105 sites with picnic tables and fire grates, $20 per night, drinking water, restrooms with flush toilets. Pets welcome. The campground can accommodate RVs up to 21 feet; a few sites can accommodate RVs up to 35 feet. There is a 14-day stay limit. Sites are available on a first-come, first-served basis; reservations are not accepted.

Hoh Campground

Located about 87 miles southwest of Port Angeles via US-101 and Upper Hoh Road. Open year-round, 78 sites with picnic tables and fire grates, $20 per night, drinking water, restrooms with flush toilets. Pets welcome. The campground can accommodate RVs up to 21 feet; a few sites can accommodate RVs up to 35 feet. There is a 14-day stay limit. Sites are available on a first-come, first-served basis; reservations are not accepted.

Kalaloch Campground

Located about 35 miles south of Forks on US-101. Open year-round, 170 sites with picnic tables and fire grates, $22 per night, drinking water, restrooms with flush toilets, dump station. Pets welcome. The campground can accommodate RVs up to 21 feet; a few sites can accommodate RVs up to 35 feet. There is a 7-day stay limit in summer, 14 days remainder of year. Reservations are accepted and can be made online at recreation.gov or by calling 877-444-6777.

Mora Campground

Located 14 miles west of Forks on Mora Road via SR-110. Open year-round, 94 sites with picnic tables and fire grates, $20 per night, drinking water, restrooms with flush toilets, dump station. Pets welcome. The campground can accommodate RVs up to 21 feet; a few sites can accommodate RVs up to 35 feet. There is a 14-day stay limit. Sites are available on a first-come, first-served basis; reservations are not accepted.

Ozette Campground

Located about 24 miles southwest of Sekiu via SR-112 and Hoko Ozette Road. Open year-round, 15 sites with picnic tables and fire grates, $20 per night, potable water, pit toilets. Pets welcome. The campground can accommodate RVs up to 21 feet. There is a 14-day stay limit. Sites are available on a first-come, first-served basis; reservations are not accepted.

Sol Duc Campground

Located about 40 miles southwest of Port Angeles via US-101 and Sol Duc River Road. Open year-round, 82 sites with picnic tables and fire grates, $20 per night, drinking water, restrooms with flush toilets, dump station. Pit toilets and no water in off-season. Pets welcome. The campground can accommodate RVs up to 21 feet; a few sites can accommodate RVs up to 35 feet. There is a 14-day stay limit. Reservations are accepted and can be made online at recreation.gov or by calling 877-444-6777.

South Beach Campground

Located about 38 miles south of Forks on US-101. Open mid-May to mid-September, 55 sites with picnic tables and fire grates, $15 per night, no potable water, restrooms with flush toilets. Pets welcome. The campground can accommodate RVs up to 21 feet; a few sites can accommodate RVs up to 35 feet. There is a 14-day stay limit. Sites are available on a first-come, first-served basis; reservations are not accepted.

Staircase Campground

Located about 16 miles northwest of Hoodsport via SR-119. Open year-round, 49 sites with picnic tables and fire grates, $20 per night, drinking water, restrooms with flush toilets. Pit toilets and no water in off-season. Pets welcome. The campground can accommodate RVs up to 21 feet; a few sites can accommodate RVs up to 35 feet. There is a 14-day stay limit. Sites are available on a first-come, first-served basis; reservations are not accepted.

West Virginia

MARYLAND

Chesapeake & Ohio Canal NHP (see Maryland)

81

PENNSYLVANIA

VIRGINIA

50

33

68

219

Leadsville

Morgantown

79

50

33

Parkersburg

WEST VIRGINIA

50

Sutton

219

19

79

New River Gorge NR

64

Gauley River NRA

64
77

Beckley

77

77

Charleston

64

OHIO

KENTUCKY

5

4

3

2

1

D

C

B

A

West Virginia Parks

	Map	Auto Touring	Biking	Boating	Climbing	Fishing	Hiking	Horseback Riding	Hunting	Snow Skiing	Swimming	Visitor Center	Wildlife Viewing
Chesapeake & Ohio Canal NHP - **see Maryland**	C5		•	•	•	•	•	•				•	•
Gauley River National Recreation Area	B2			•			•	•					
New River Gorge National River	A2	•	•	•	•	•	•	•	•			•	•

PARK DETAILS

Gauley River National Recreation Area

PO Box 246
Glen Jean, WV 25846
Phone: 304-465-0508

Description

The Gauley River National Recreation Area protects 25 miles of free-flowing Gauley River and five miles of the Meadow River. Every September, as water is released from Summersville Dam, whitewater enthusiasts come to enjoy rafting on the river, which contains several class V+ rapids. More than 100,000 people come to the park every year.

Information

There is no visitor center within the park but information is available at the nearby Canyon Rim Visitor Center within New River Gorge National River. The visitor center is located along US-19 and is open daily year-round except on Thanksgiving, Christmas, and New Year's Day. Hours are typically 9am to 5pm.

Fees & Season

The park is open all year. No entrance fee is charged.

Directions

Gauley River National Recreation Area is in southern West Virginia near Summersville. The main entrance to the park is off US-19 via SR-129 to Summersville Dam then second left after crossing the dam.

RV CAMPING

Gauley Tailwaters Campground

Located west of US-19 off SR-139 below Summersville Dam. Open year-round, 18 sites with picnic tables and fire grates, free, no water, vault toilets. Pets welcome. The campground cannot accommodate large RVs. There is a 14-day stay limit. Sites are available on a first-come, first-served basis; reservations are not accepted.

PARK DETAILS

New River Gorge National River

PO Box 246
Glen Jean, WV 25846
Phone: 304-465-0508

Description

Established in 1978, New River Gorge National River encompasses over 70,000 acres of land along 53 miles of the New River from Bluestone Dam to Hawk's Nest Lake. New River is a rugged whitewater river flowing northward through the deepest and longest river gorge in the Appalachian Mountains. Over one million people visit the park each year to float the river, hike along the many park trails, or ride a bike along an old railroad grade.

Information

Information is available from several visitor centers throughout the park. Canyon Rim Visitor Center is located off US-129 in Lansing near the New River Gorge Bridge. The visitor center is open daily year-round from 9am to 5pm; it closes on Thanksgiving, Christmas, and New Year's Day. It features an exhibit room filled with photographs and exhibits of the people, towns, and industry of the area. Other displays focus on the recreation and natural history of the area. There is also an orientation video.

Grandview Visitor Center overlooks the deepest part of the gorge, some 1,400 feet above the river. The center is open in summer from Noon to 5pm. It may open intermittently later into fall depending on staffing. The visitor center and overlook is along CR-9 about five miles north of I-64 Exit 129 or Exit 1295B.

Sandstone Visitor Center is located just north of the I-64 and SR-20 interchange at Exit 139. Features include exhibits of the park's natural and cultural history, a 12-minute orientation video, and a publication sales area. The visitor center is open daily from 9am to 5pm from April through November. From December through March, the visitor center is open Friday through Monday. It closes on Thanksgiving, Christmas, and New Year's Day.

Thurmond Depot Visitor Center is open seasonally and is located inside a restored railroad depot. The depot once served the Chesapeake & Ohio Railway and is currently used by Amtrak. The depot is about 18 miles northeast of Beckley via US-19 and CR-25. The county road is narrow and winding; it is not recommended for RVs and trailers.

Fees & Season
The park is open all year. No entrance fee is charged.

Directions
New River Gorge National River is in southern West Virginia near Beckley. Portions of the park are accessible from various highways including I-64, US-19, US-60, and SR-41.

RV CAMPING

Army Camp Campground
Located about 12 miles northeast of Beckley via SR-41 and Army Camp Rd. Open year-round, 11 sites with picnic tables and fire grates, free, no potable water, vault toilets. Pets welcome. The campground can accommodate large RVs at some sites. Access road is narrow in places. There is a 14-day stay limit. Sites are available on a first-come, first-served basis; reservations are not accepted.

Glade Creek Campground
Located near Prince about six miles southeast of SR-41 at the end of Glade Creek Road. Open year-round, five sites with picnic tables and fire grates, free, no potable water, vault toilets. Pets welcome. The campground can accommodate small/medium RVs. There is a 14-day stay limit. Sites are available on a first-come, first-served basis; reservations are not accepted.

Grandview Sandbar Campground
Located near Prince about one mile east of SR-41 on Glade Creek Road. Open all year, 10 sites with picnic tables and fire grates, free, no potable water, vault toilets. Pets welcome. The campground can accommodate small/medium RVs. There is a 14-day stay limit. Sites are available on a first-come, first-served basis; reservations are not accepted.

Meadow Creek Campground
Located off I-64 Exit 139 about two miles west of the Sandstone Visitor Center. Open all year, five sites with picnic tables and fire grates, free, no potable water, vault toilets. Pets welcome. The campground can accommodate large RVs. There is a 14-day stay limit. Sites are available on a first-come, first-served basis; reservations are not accepted.

War Ridge/Backus Mountain Campground
Located about seven miles east of Prince via SR-41, Backus Mountain Road, and Fayette Road. Open all year, eight sites with picnic tables and fire grates, free, no potable water, vault toilets. Pets welcome. The campground can accommodate small RVs only. There is a 14-day stay limit. Sites are available on a first-come, first-served basis; reservations are not accepted.

Wyoming

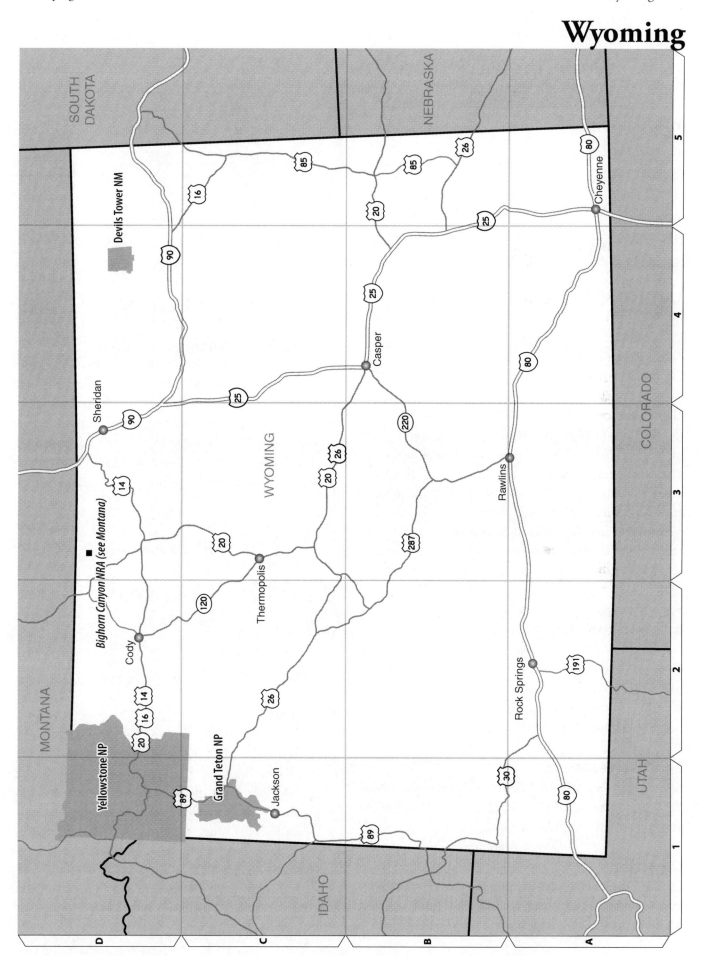

SOUTH DAKOTA

NEBRASKA

Cheyenne

Devils Tower NM

Sheridan

WYOMING

Casper

COLORADO

Bighorn Canyon NRA (see Montana)

Cody

Thermopolis

Rawlins

Rock Springs

MONTANA

Yellowstone NP

Grand Teton NP

Jackson

IDAHO

UTAH

Wyoming Parks

	Map	Auto Touring	Biking	Boating	Climbing	Fishing	Hiking	Horseback Riding	Hunting	Snow Skiing	Swimming	Visitor Center	Wildlife Viewing
Bighorn Canyon National Recreation Area - *see Montana*	D3	•	•	•		•	•		•			•	• •
Devils Tower National Monument	D4				•		•					•	•
Grand Teton National Park	C1	•	•	•	•	•	•	•				•	•
Yellowstone National Park	D1	•	•	•		•	•	•			•	•	•

PARK DETAILS

Devils Tower National Monument

PO Box 10
Devils Tower, WY 82714
Phone: 307-467-5283 x635

Description

Devils Tower National Monument was established in 1906 as the nation's first national monument. The 1,346-acre park features the nearly vertical Devils Tower, which rises 1,267 feet above the Belle Fourche River. The site is considered sacred to the Lakota and other tribes that have a connections to the area. More than 400,000 people come to the park each year; many to climb this geologic feature protruding out of the prairie.

Information

Information is available from the Devils Tower Visitor Center located at the end of the park road at the base of the Tower. The visitor center is open spring through fall; hours vary by season. Features include exhibits of the natural and cultural history and book sales.

Fees & Season

The park is open all year except on Christmas and New Year's Day. An entrance fee of $25 per vehicle is charged and is valid for seven days.

Directions

Devils Tower National Monument is in northeast Wyoming about 27 miles northwest of Sundance and 32 miles northeast of Moorcroft. I-90 travelers can exit in Sundance or Moorcroft and follow US-14 to SR-24 and the park entrance.

RV CAMPING

Belle Fourche Campground

Located about one mile from the park entrance. Open spring to fall, 43 sites with picnic tables and fire grates, $20 per night, drinking water, restrooms with flush toilets. Pets welcome. The campground can accommodate RVs up to 35 feet. There is a 14-day stay limit. Sites are available on a first-come, first-served basis; reservations are not accepted.

PARK DETAILS

Grand Teton National Park

PO Drawer 170
Moose, WY 83012
Phone: 307-739-3399

Description

Established in 1929, Grand Teton National Park protects nearly 310,000 acres of mountains, valleys, lakes, rivers, and an abundance of varied wildlife. The park's namesake peak stands at 13,770 feet and is a prominent feature. Over two hundred miles of trails meander throughout the wilderness. More than three million people come the park every year to enjoy camping, hiking, boating, fishing, biking, and other outdoor activities. Peak visitation occurs during summer, especially July and August.

Scenic Drives

The Jenny Lake Scenic Drive skirts the eastern shore of Jenny Lake and provides spectacular views of the peaks. Access the scenic drive from Teton Park Road at North Jenny Lake Junction. Drive west toward the mountains and turn south (left) onto the one-way scenic drive. The road returns to Teton Park Road not far from the Jenny Lake Visitor Center.

Signal Mountain Summit Road climbs 800 feet and provides panoramic views of the Teton Range, Jackson Hile valley, and Jackson Lake. Two overlooks provide valley views. The road is accessed from Teton Park Road about nine miles north of Jenny Lake Visitor Center. The road is steep and narrow, trailers are prohibited.

Information

Information is available from the following visitor centers:

Colter Bay Visitor Center is located adjacent to Jackson Lake about 25 miles north of Moose. It is generally open from mid-May to early October. Summer hours are 8am to 7pm; spring and fall hours are 8am to 5pm. From June through September, craft demonstrations and museum tours are offered.

Jenny Lake Visitor Center is about eight miles north of Moose along Teton Park Road. It is generally open from mid-May to late September. Summer hours are 8am to 7pm; spring and fall hours are 8am to 5pm. Features include geology exhibits and a relief map of the park.

The Craig Thomas Discovery & Visitor Center, also known as the Moose Visitor Center, is 12 miles north of Jackson on Teton Park Road, just west of US-26. It is generally open March through October. Summer hours are 8am to 7pm; late spring and fall hours 8am to 5pm. In March and April, the hours are 10am to 4pm. The Discovery Center features natural history exhibits, a relief map of the park, and an introductory video.

Fees & Season

The park is open all year but some road closures in winter limit access to some areas of the park. An entrance fee of $35 per vehicle is charged and is valid for seven days. The entrance fee is also valid for nearby John D. Rockefeller, Jr. Memorial Parkway. It does not provide entrance into Yellowstone National Park, which has a separate entrance fee.

Directions

Grand Teton National Park is in northwest Wyoming about five miles north of Jackson. US-26 and US-89 pass through the park.

RV CAMPING

Colter Bay Campground

Located about 28 miles north of Moose off US-89. Open late May through September, 162 RV sites ($31 per night), 13 sites with electric hookups ($53.00 per night), picnic tables and fire grates at each site, drinking water, restrooms with flush toilets, dump station. Showers and coin-operated laundry services nearby. Pets welcome. The campground can accommodate RVs up to 45 feet. There is a 14-day stay limit. Sites are available on a first-come, first-served basis; reservations are not accepted. Sites generally fill daily between Noon and 3pm from mid-June to mid-August.

Colter Bay RV Park

Located adjacent to the Colter Bay Campground. Open mid-May to early October, 103 pull-through sites with full hookups ($71 per night), 9 back-in sites ($61 per night, 30 foot max total length), picnic tables, drinking water, restrooms with flush toilets, showers, laundry facility. No open fires permitted. Pets welcome. The campground can accommodate large RVs. There is a 14-day stay limit. Reservations are accepted and can be made online at gtlc.com or by calling 307-543-3100. This campground is the most popular for RV camping. Reservations for June through September fill quickly. It is recommended you make reservations prior to January 1st for the best availability.

Gros Ventre Campground

Located about ten miles northeast of Jackson via US-89 and Gros Ventre Road. Open early May to early October, 282 sites ($29 per night), 36 sites with electric hookups ($53 per night), picnic tables and fire grates at each site, drinking water, restrooms with flush toilets, dump station. Pets welcome. The campground can accommodate RVs up to 45 feet. There is a 14-day stay limit. Sites are available on a first-come, first-served basis; reservations are not accepted. Sites generally fill daily between Noon and 5pm from mid-June to mid-August.

Headwaters Campground & RV Sites

Located along US-89 five miles outside of the park but within the John D. Rockefeller, Jr. Memorial Parkway. Open mid-May to late September, 97 RV sites with full hookups, $74 per night, picnic tables and fire grates at each site, drinking water, restrooms with flush toilets, showers, laundry facilities. Pets welcome. The campground can accommodate RVs up to 45 feet. There is a 14-day stay limit. Reservations are accepted and can be made online at gtlc.com or by calling 307-543-2861. Sites generally fill daily between Noon and 4pm from mid-June to early September.

Lizard Creek Campground

Located about 32 miles north of Moose via US-89. Open mid-June to early September, 60 sites with picnic tables and fire grates, $30 per night, drinking water, restrooms with flush toilets. Pets welcome. The campground can accommodate RVs up to 30 feet. There is a 14-day stay limit. Sites are available on a first-come, first-served basis; reservations are not accepted. Campground typically fills by mid-afternoon from mid-June to mid-August.

Signal Mountain Campground

Located 18 miles north of Moose along Teton Park Road. Open mid-May to mid-October, 57 non-electric sites ($32 per night), 24 sites with electric ($54 per night), picnic tables and fire grates at each site, drinking water, restrooms with flush toilets, dump station. Showers and laundry services available. A general store is located at nearby Signal Mountain Lodge. Pets welcome. The campground can accommodate RVs up to 30 feet. There is a 14-day stay limit. Sites are available on a first-come, first-served basis; reservations are not accepted. The campground typically fills by mid-morning from mid-June to mid-August.

PARK DETAILS

Yellowstone National Park

PO Box 168
Yellowstone National Park, WY 82190
Phone: 307-344-7381

Description

Yellowstone National Park was established in 1872 as the first national park in America and the world. It protects more than two million acres of mountains, meadows, and lakes. There are more geysers and hot springs here than anywhere in the world. More than four million people come to the park annually. Visitation is highest in summer from June through August.

Information

Ten visitor centers and information stations are found throughout the park. Each location has information, exhibits and rangers available to answer questions. Albright Visitor Center is five miles south of the North Entrance in Mammoth Hot Springs and is open daily year-round with extended hours during summer. Canyon Visitor Education Center is open daily late spring through mid-fall and is located in the Canyon Village area. Fishing Bridge Visitor Center is one mile off the Grand Loop Road on East Entrance Road and is open May to September. Grant Visitor Center is open May to September and is on the shore of West Thumb of Yellowstone Lake in Grant Village. Old Faithful Visitor Education Center is on Grand Loop Road 16 miles south of Madison Junction. It is open daily throughout the year with two, month-long closed periods in the spring and fall. Hours of operation for all visitor centers vary by season.

Fees & Season

Park roads between the North and Northeast entrances are open year-round. Other park entrances and roads are closed in winter. Various facilities begin closing for the winter season in September. An entrance fee of $35 per vehicle is charged and is valid for seven days.

Directions

Yellowstone National Park is located in northwest Wyoming; small portions extend into Idaho and Montana. The park can be accessed from US-20, US-89, and US-212.

RV CAMPING

Bridge Bay Campground

Concession-operated campground located across the road from Yellowstone Lake about 29 miles west of the park's eastern entrance. Open mid-May to late September, 432 sites with picnic tables and fire grates, $25.25 per night, drinking water, restrooms with flush toilets, dump station. Generators permitted (60db limit). Pets welcome. The campground can accommodate RVs up to 40 feet at some sites. There is a 14-day stay limit. Reservations are accepted and can be made online at www.YellowstoneNationalParkLodges.com or by calling 307-344-7311. Bridge Bay Marina is just outside the campground entrance and offers boat tours, rental boats, guided fishing trips, and other services.

Canyon Campground

Concession-operated campground located in one of the most popular sections of the park, Canyon Village. Open late May to late September, 270 sites with picnic tables and fire grates, $30 per night, drinking water, restrooms with flush toilets, showers, laundry facilities, dump station. Generators permitted (60db limit). Pets welcome. The campground can accommodate RVs up to 40 feet at some sites. There is a 14-day stay limit. Reservations are accepted and can be made online at www.YellowstoneNationalParkLodges.com or by calling 307-344-7311.

Fishing Bridge RV Park

Concession-operated campground located about 25 miles west of the park's east entrance along US-20. Open mid-May to early September, 340 sites with full (50 amp) hookups, $47.75 per night, drinking water, restrooms with flush toilets, showers, laundry facilities, dump station, general store nearby. Campfires are prohibited in the campground. Generators permitted (60db limit). Pets welcome. The campground can accommodate RVs up to 40 feet. There is no length of stay limit at this campground. Reservations are accepted and can be made online at www.YellowstoneNationalParkLodges.com or by calling 307-344-7311. Because grizzly bears frequent the area, only hard sided RVs are permitted; tents and tent campers are prohibited. Discount cards are not accepted at this campground. The campground will be closed during the 2019 season for renovation.

Grant Village Campground

Concession-operated campground located on the southwest shore of Yellowstone Lake. Open June to mid-September, 430 sites with picnic tables and fire grates, $30 per night, drinking water, restrooms with flush toilets, showers, laundry facilities, dump station. A general store is nearby. Generators permitted (60db limit). Pets welcome. The campground can accommodate RVs up to 40 feet at some sites. There is a 14-day stay limit. Reservations are accepted and can be made online at www.YellowstoneNationalParkLodges.com or by calling 307-344-7311.

Indian Creek Campground

Located along US-89 about 13 miles south of the park's north entrance. Open early June to mid-September, 70 sites with picnic tables and fire grates, $15 per night, drinking water, vault toilets. Generators are prohibited. Pets welcome. The campground can accommodate RVs up to 35 feet at 10 sites; 35 sites have a maximum length of 30 feet. There is a 14-day stay limit. Sites are available on a first-come, first-served basis; reservations are not accepted. The campground typically fills by early morning; plan ahead to obtain a site.

Lewis Lake Campground

Located about eight miles from the park's south entrance on US-89. Open mid-June through October, 85 sites with picnic tables and fire grates, $15 per night, drinking water, vault toilets. Generators are prohibited. Pets welcome. RVs and vehicle/trailer combinations longer than 25 feet are prohibited. There is a 14-day stay limit. Sites are available on a first-come, first-served basis; reservations are not accepted. The campground typically fills by early morning; plan ahead to obtain a site.

Madison Campground

Concession-operated campground located about 14 miles east of the park's west entrance near Madison Junction. Open May to mid-October, 278 sites with picnic tables and fire grates, $25.25 per night, drinking water, restrooms with flush toilets. Generators permitted (60db limit). Pets welcome. The campground can accommodate RVs up to 40 feet at some sites. There is a 14-day stay limit. Reservations are accepted and can be made online at www.YellowstoneNationalParkLodges.com or by calling 307-344-7311.

Mammoth Hot Springs Campground

Located in the northern part of the park about five miles south of Gardiner, Montana, and the park's north entrance. Open all year, 85 sites with picnic tables and fire grates, $20 per night, drinking water, restrooms with flush toilets, vault toilets. Generators permitted (60db limit). Pets welcome. Most sites are pull-through and can accommodate large RVs. There is a 14-day stay limit. Sites are available on a first-come, first-served basis; reservations are not accepted. The campground typically fills by early morning; plan ahead to obtain a site.

Norris Campground

Located about 25 miles south of the park's north entrance. Open late May to late September, 111 sites with picnic tables and fire grates, $20 per night, drinking water, restrooms with flush toilets. Generators permitted (60db limit). Pets welcome. The campground can accommodate RVs up to 50 feet at two sites and 30 feet at five sites. There is a 14-day stay limit. Sites are available on a first-come, first-served basis; reservations are not accepted. The campground typically fills by early morning; plan ahead to obtain a site.

Pebble Creek Campground

Located along US-212 about nine miles from the park's northeast entrance. Open mid-June to late September, 27 sites with picnic tables and fire grates, $15 per night, drinking water, vault toilets. Generators are prohibited. Pets welcome. The campground can accommodate large RVs at some pull-through sites. There is a 14-day stay limit. Sites are available on a first-come, first-served basis; reservations are not accepted. The campground typically fills by early morning; plan ahead to obtain a site.

Slough Creek Campground

Located off US-212 about 24 miles from the park's northeast entrance. Open mid-June to early October, 16 sites with picnic tables and fire grates, $15 per night, drinking water, vault toilets. Generators are prohibited. Pets welcome. The campground can accommodate RVs and vehicle/trailer combinations up to 30 feet at some sites; it is recommended you walk through first to assess sites. There is a 14-day stay limit. Sites are available on a first-come, first-served basis; reservations are not accepted. The campground typically fills by early morning; plan ahead to obtain a site.

Tower Fall Campground

Located on Grand Loop Road about 25 miles from the park's north entrance. Open late May to late September, 31 sites with picnic tables and fire grates, $15 per night, drinking water, vault toilets. Generators prohibited. Pets welcome. The campground cannot accommodate RVs and vehicle/trailer combinations longer than 30 feet. There is a 14-day stay limit. Sites are available on a first-come, first-served basis; reservations are not accepted. The campground typically fills by early morning; plan ahead to obtain a site.

Appendix A

America the Beautiful Passes

Frequent visitors to National Park Service areas can receive significant savings with the America the Beautiful Senior Pass or Access Pass, recreation passes issued by the federal government. Both of these passes are honored at National Park Service campgrounds. The passes provide a 50 percent discount on fees charged for facilities and services such as camping, swimming, parking, boat launching, and tours. In some cases where use fees are charged, only the pass signee will be given the 50 percent price reduction. It generally does not cover or reduce special recreation permit fees or fees charged by concessionaires.

Senior Pass

This pass is for citizens of the United States who are 62 or older. The cost for a lifetime Senior Pass is $80; proof of age must be shown. It is a lifetime entrance pass to national parks, monuments, historic sites, recreation areas, and national wildlife refuges that charge an entrance fee. The Senior Pass admits the pass signee and any accompanying passengers in a private vehicle. Senior Pass holders get 50% off camping fees at Corps-managed campgrounds. An annual Senior Pass is also available for $20.

Access Pass

This pass is for citizens of the United States who are blind or permanently disabled. The Access Pass is free; proof of medically determined permanent disability or eligibility for receiving benefits under federal law must be shown. It is a lifetime entrance pass to national parks, monuments, historic sites, recreation areas, and national wildlife refuges that charge an entrance fee. The passport admits the pass signee and any accompanying passengers in a private vehicle. Access Pass holders get 50% off camping fees at Corps-managed campgrounds.

Where to Get A Pass

A Senior Pass or Access Pass can be obtained in person, online, or by mail. To learn more or to order a pass, go online to https://store.usgs.gov/senior-pass.

As of January 1, 2007, the America the Beautiful Senior Pass and Access Pass replaced the Golden Age and Golden Access Passports issued before 2007. Although not sold anymore, existing Golden Age and Golden Access Passports remain valid for the lifetime of pass holders.

Appendix B

Designation of National Park Service Units

The National Park Service manages over 400 areas (or units) covering more than 84 million acres in all 50 states, the District of Columbia, and U.S. possessions. These areas include national parks, seashores, battlefields, and historic sites nationwide. They offer a wide variety of outdoor recreation and educational experiences for the visitor.

Although the National Park Service is best known for its great scenic parks, more than half of the areas preserve places that commemorate persons, events, and activities important in our nation's history. These range from archeological sites associated with prehistoric Indian civilizations to sites related to the lives of modern Americans.

The numerous designations within the National Park Service can be confusing to visitors. Listed below is a description of the different types of areas managed by the National Park Service.

- **National Park**: These are generally large natural places having a wide variety of attributes, at times including significant historic assets. Hunting, mining and consumptive activities are not authorized.

- **National Monument**: The Antiquities Act of 1906 authorized the President to declare by public proclamation landmarks, structures, and other objects of historic or scientific interest situated on lands owned or controlled by the government to be national monuments.

- **National Preserve**: National preserves are areas having characteristics associated with national parks, but in which Congress has permitted continued public hunting, trapping, oil/gas exploration and extraction. Many existing national preserves, without sport hunting, would qualify for national park designation.

- **National Historic Site**: Usually, a national historic site contains a single historical feature that was directly associated with its subject. Derived from the Historic Sites Act of 1935, a number of historic sites were established by secretaries of the Interior, but most have been authorized by acts of Congress.

- **National Historical Park**: This designation generally applies to historic parks that extend beyond single properties or buildings.

- **National Memorial**: A national memorial is commemorative of a historic person or episode; it need not occupy a site historically connected with its subject.

- **National Battlefield**: This general title includes national battlefield, national battlefield park, national battlefield site, and national military park. In 1958, an NPS committee recommended national battlefield as the single title for all such park lands.

- **National Cemetery**: There are presently 14 national cemeteries in the National Park System, all of which are administered in conjunction with an associated unit and are not accounted for separately.

- **National Recreation Area**: Twelve national recreation areas (NRAs) in the system are centered on large reservoirs and emphasize water-based recreation. Five other NRAs are located near major population centers. Such urban parks combine scarce open spaces with the preservation of significant historic resources and important natural areas in a location that can provide outdoor recreation for large numbers of people.

- **National Seashore:** Ten national seashores have been established on the Atlantic, Gulf and Pacific coasts; some are developed and some relatively primitive. Hunting is allowed at many of these sites.

- **National Lakeshore:** National lakeshores, all on the Great Lakes, closely parallel the seashores in character and use.

- **National River:** There are several variations to this category: national river and recreation area, national scenic river, wild river, etc. The first was authorized in 1964 and others were established following passage of the Wild and Scenic Rivers Act of 1968.

- **National Parkway:** The title parkway refers to a roadway and the parkland paralleling the roadway. All were intended for scenic motoring along a protected corridor and often connect cultural sites.

- **National Trail:** National scenic trails and national historic trails are the titles given to these linear parklands (over 3,600 miles) authorized under the National Trails System Act of 1968.

- **Other Designations:** Some units of the National Park System bear unique titles or combinations of titles, like the White House and Prince William Forest Park.

Appendix C

Visiting Parks With Your Pets

Pets are generally permitted in National Park Service areas but must be restrained either on a leash not exceeding 6 feet in length, caged, or crated at all times. Park Superintendents and Managers have the discretion to further restrict areas open to pets (i.e. trails, buildings, and campgrounds may be off limits).

Restrictions on pets in parks are as much to protect your pet as to protect park resources. The following are some of the reasons parks give for regulating the presence of pets:

- When a loose pet chases a squirrel or raccoon, the wild animal's ability to survive is threatened, and when it is threatened, it may react aggressively.

- There is a strong possibility in parks such as Yellowstone that your pet could become prey for bear, coyote, owl, or other predators.

- There is a possibility of exchange of diseases between domestic animals and wildlife.

- Dogs, the most common traveling companion, are natural predators that may harass or even kill native wildlife that is protected within the park's boundaries.

- The "scent of a predator" that dogs leave behind can disrupt or alter the behavior of native animals.

- Pets may be hard to control, even on a leash, within confines of often narrow park trails and may trample or dig up fragile vegetation.

- Dog and cat feces add excessive nutrients and bacterial pollution to water, which decreases water quality and can also cause human health problems.

- Finally, lost domestic animals sometimes turn to preying on park wildlife and must be destroyed.

Some park website pages list nearby kennels where you can leave your pet during your stay in the park. You can access information on the parks you plan to visit by going to the National Parks website at nps.gov. It is always best to check with the park(s) you are planning to visit for specific information and restrictions regarding pets.

Appendix D

Free Camping Areas

The following is a list of RV campgrounds within National Park Service areas where camping is free. Some locations may only be free during certain times of the year. Check each campground for details.

Alaska

Denali National Park & Preserve
- Riley Creek Campground

Wrangell-Saint Elias National Park & Preserve
- Kendesnii Campground

Arizona

Navajo National Monument
- Sunset View Campground

Arkansas

Buffalo National River
- Erbie Campground

California

Death Valley National Park
- Wildrose Campground

Mississippi

Natchez Trace Parkway
- Jeff Busby Campground
- Rocky Springs Campground

New Mexico

El Morro National Monument
- El Morro Campground

Tennessee

Natchez Trace Parkway (see Mississippi)
- Meriwether Lewis Campground

Texas

Lake Meredith National Recreation Area
- Blue West Campground
- Fritch Fortress Campground
- Sanford-Yake Campground

Washington

North Cascades National Park
- Colonial Creek Campground
- Goodell Creek Campground
- Gorge Lake Campground
- Hozomeen Campground

West Virginia

Gauley River National Recreation Area
- Gauley Tailwaters Campground

New River Gorge National River
- Army Camp Campground
- Glade Creek Campground
- Grandview Sandbar Campground
- Meadow Creek Campground
- War Ridge/Backus Mountain Campground

Index

Made in United States
Orlando, FL
17 April 2024